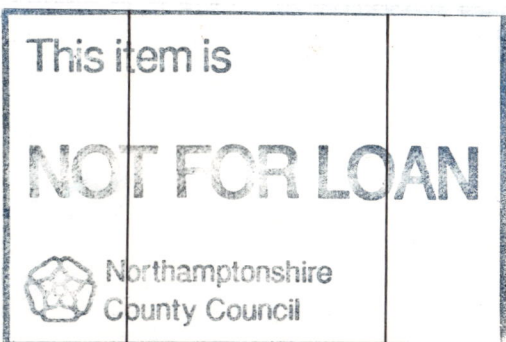

TRANSPORT RESEARCH LABORATORY
Department of Transport

STATE-OF-THE-ART REVIEW 10

PUBLIC TRANSPORT IN THIRD WORLD CITIES

by Alan Armstrong-Wright

LONDON:HMSO

 **HMSO**

HMSO publications are available from:

HMSO Publications Centre
(Mail, fax and telephone orders only)
PO Box 276, London, SW8 5DT
Telephone orders 071-873 9090
General enquiries 071-873 0011
(queuing system in operation for both numbers)
Fax orders 071-873 8200

HMSO Bookshops
49 High Holborn, London, WC1V 6HB
071-873 0011   Fax 071-873 8200 (counter service only)
258 Broad Street, Birmingham, B1 2HE
021-643 3740   Fax 021-643 6510
Southey House, 33 Wine Street, Bristol, BS1 2BQ
0272 264306   Fax 0272 294515
9-21 Princess Street, Manchester, M60 8AS
061-834 7201   Fax 061-833 0634
16 Arthur Street, Belfast, BT1 4GD
0232 238451   Fax 0232 235401
71 Lothian Road, Edinburgh, EH3 9AZ
031-228 4181   Fax 031-229 2734

HMSO's Accredited Agents
(see Yellow Pages)

and through good booksellers

Contents

1.   Introduction   1

2.   Bus services   4

3.   Articulated buses and trolleybuses   21

4.   Paratransit and taxis   25

5.   Busway transit   31

6.   Rail mass transit: Metros   38

7.   Light rail transit   50

8.   Suburban railways   58

9.   Traffic management: Impact on public transport   62

10. Fares and fare collection   70

11. Financing public transport   75

12. Institutional structures   84

13. Environmental impact of urban transport   90

14. Urban transport: The future   96

15. Bibliography   104

Preface

The number of urban dwellers in the Third World is rapidly approaching 2000 million. Most rely heavily on some form of public transport for their everyday activities. With such vast numbers affected, it is not surprising to find the state of public transport a raging issue throughout the Third World. In addition to the well being of its users, public transport plays a vital role in the productivity of cities which in turn has a direct bearing on national economies.

This review has been undertaken in recognition of the importance and magnitude of public transport in the Third World cities. Its purpose is to provide a concise and comprehensive insight of the subject, with illustrative case studies. In particular, it aims to provide background information for:

- *aid agencies* seeking to identify opportunities to assist Third World countries with projects likely to achieve wide benefits, particularly to low income groups,
- *researchers* to identify areas of useful research, (eg for masters degrees and doctorates), and as a starting point for more in-depth research in order to provide informed and objective advice for decision makers,
- *businessmen* exploring markets for their products, services or investments in public transport,
- *Third World authorities* planning improvements and interested in the approaches adopted to problems in other developing cities,
- *consultants* embarking on studies and in need of a briefing of the general situation of public transport in Third World cities.

The review covers each of the common modes of public transport, together with some of the main variants such as trolleybuses, paratransit and busways, in separate chapters. It also covers subjects which influence or are affected by the state of public transport: for example its impact on the environment. The review describes the situation as it exists, and so avoids discussing untried schemes that may be in the pipe-line. However, as needs be, the chapter on the future of public transport involves an element of prediction. The review also avoids prescribing solutions, this being more appropriately the role of policy studies and guidelines (eg Urban Transport: A World Bank Policy Study).

The review is based on comprehensive studies of bus services, light rail transit and metros in developing cities undertaken by TRL, Overseas Unit, and the examination of public transport in some 65 cities in the Third World by the author as a World Bank staff member and as a consultant. Use also has been made of extensive reference material. General works of reference together with selected publications and papers of broad interest are listed in the bibliography.

In this review, the Third World is considered to comprise countries with comparatively low levels of earnings and industrialisation. It includes most of Africa, South and Central America, and Asia excluding Japan. The review makes brief references to other countries, such as Hongkong and Singapore, which have economies and levels of earnings more akin to those in industrialized countries. These have been included because they provide a useful indication of technology that may be appropriate to Third World countries following similar rapid development trends.

Acknowledgements

The author wishes to acknowledge his appreciation of the valuable assistance in the preparation of this review provided by the TRL Overseas Unit,(Unit Head: J S Yerrell) in particular Philip Fouracre and Geoff Gardner; Roger Allport (Halcrow, Fox and Associates), Richard Barrett, John Flora and Richard Scurfield (The World Bank), and the many officials, transport operators and consultants around the world who have provided information on their public transport systems, studies and projects.

Finally, the author wishes to express his thanks to his wife for her unstinted support in the preparation of this review, including the proof reading of the drafts.

1 INTRODUCTION

With very few exceptions, urban transport in the Third World is characterised by rapid growth in demand which has overwhelmed transport capacity. Road congestion is wide spread, public transport is overloaded and, due to a lack of maintenance, roads are often in a poor state of repair. The ability to cope with these conditions has been strictly limited due to a lack of resources and low earnings. The level of per capita earnings (GNP per capita) in Third World countries is on average only US$700 per annum - in many it is less than US$200. It is only a fraction of that in industrialised countries where the average is US$14,500, and accounts for the very considerable differences between the standards of services that are affordable. In many Third World countries economic growth has at best been stagnant and in some, particularly in Africa, has declined. Oil crisis has followed oil crisis, drought has followed drought, and in some countries, despite much outside aid, economic development has been stifled by internal strife and instability. Nevertheless, there are many remarkable examples of urban authorities and communities rising above these difficulties. With very considerable resourcefulness they have gone a long way towards meeting what must at times seem to be impossible demands. Large scale counter-measures have been pursued, but because of the rapid growth in demand, lasting improvements have been elusive. In fact, most face a worsening situation.

On average, the urban populations of the Third World are growing at about 6 per cent per year. Well above average increases are being experienced in China where the annual growth rate is 11 per cent, and in Africa where for example, growth rates of 11 per cent are found in Tanzania and Mozambique, and close to 9 per cent in Malawi, Burundi and Kenya. While the urban population in India is growing at below average at 4 per cent, the annual increase in absolute terms is about 9 million - equivalent to a city the size of Paris being created every year! The total Third World urban population was estimated at 800 million in 1980 and is expected to have more than doubled to 2000 million by year 2000. A large part of this urban growth can be expected to take place in low-income suburbs on the periphery of urban centres.

These increases in urban populations have in turn resulted in massive increases in the demand for transport. Other factors adding significantly to the level of demand are the spread of urban areas leading to longer and more motorised trips, increased commercial and industrial activity and a greater propensity to travel where incomes have risen. In most cities, because of these factors demand for public transport in particular, has grown even faster than the population. In addition, in almost all cities the growth in demand has out-stripped the growth in budget revenues. This has had a serious impact on public sector services which generally rely on subsidies. Rarely can subsidies be increased sufficiently to cope with the increasing costs of existing services, let alone expanded operations. As a result, in many cities public sector services are deteriorating and are quite unable to provide effective expansion in the face of increasing demand. On the other hand, while private sector services generally have been better able to cope, in many cities their expansion has been inhibited by a lack of access to funding and in some cases by undue regulation.

The modal share of urban transport trips (modal split) is subject to very wide variations between urban areas even within the same country. However, studies undertaken by the World Bank indicate that, as a rough guide, motorised modal split can be expected to fall within the following ranges:

buses and minibuses 50 - 70 per cent
paratransit   5 - 20 per cent
rail (where available) 10 - 20 per cent
private cars and taxis 15 - 30 per cent

The traffic composition in the centre of Jakarta (Plate 1.1) is typical of that found in large Third World cities.

Plate 1.1   Mid-day rush in Jakarta: typical modal split

There are a number of notable exceptions. For example, the share of buses in most Chinese cities is well above 80 per cent, with negligible use of private cars. The rail share in Bombay at over 30 per cent is exceptionally high, as is the paratransit share in Manila (jeepneys) at well above 50 per cent.

Unlike industrial countries, most trips in developing countries are made in some form of public transport - or on foot. Generally the use of private cars is comparatively very low, but is steadily growing in all but the lowest income countries. Table 1.1 illustrates the level of car ownership in a range of Third World cities compared with New York, London and Stuttgart.

TABLE 1.1
Private car ownership: city comparisons

City	Private cars per 1000 pop.
Shanghai	2
Beijing	9
Lagos	15
Bombay	20
Seoul	31
Jakarta	44
Nairobi	50
Bangkok	87
Sao Paulo	145
New York	218
London	318
Stuttgart	442

In most Third World conurbations public transport is provided by a very wide variety of buses and minibuses at different levels of technology. These are greatly supplemented by a mass of paratransit vehicles such as shared taxis, converted pickups, vans and motor scooters (auto-rickshaws) and pedal rickshaws. Most cities also have many taxis available for individual use. In a few cities, priority is given to public transport by the provision of bus-only lanes and segregated rights-of-way.

In some cities, part of the demand is met by suburban railways. However, the provision of rail mass transit (metros) and light rail transit (LRT) is comparatively rare. Even in cities with extensive metros, such as Seoul and Mexico City, the majority of public transport trips are made in buses.

In addition to public transport vehicles and private cars, traffic in Third World cities often includes a high proportion of freight and service trucks and vans and, in some cases, slow moving animal and manually drawn vehicles. In some cities, such as Karachi, motor cycles and scooters out-number cars. Pedal cycles are particulary prevalent in cities in China.

While traffic volumes are usually below the theoretical capacity of the roadways, congestion is often extensive due to poor intersection lay-outs and a lack of traffic control coupled with indiscriminate parking and street trading. The situation is often exacerbated by highly peaked demand with as much as 15 per cent of passenger flow occurring during the morning and evening peak hours. However, despite the very obvious advantages, load spreading through various means of staggered working and school hours is found in only a few cities. Measures in Seoul to advance school hours by 30 minutes and delay working hours by 30 minutes are expected to cut peak hour demand almost in half.

2 BUS SERVICES

Bus services are the dominant mode of motorised transport in Third World cities. Because of low incomes for the majority of inhabitants, buses provide the only mode of transport that they can afford. Buses and minibuses also dominate because generally they are at a level of technology compatible with local experience and facilities. Fares generally range from 10 to 25 US cents for an average 5km trip. Even so, for some low income passengers this may result in expenditure on transport as high as 30 per cent of household income. Hence the excessive walking that takes place in some cities. For example, in Nairobi 25 per cent of commuters walk to work, some as much as 10km each way.

Bus services generally comprise a mixture of conventional medium to large buses; adapted trucks ("Mammy Wagons") and minibuses (Plate 2.1). While bus designs vary considerably most are typically single deck two-axle vehicles powered by front mounted direct injection diesel engines. They generally have two doors and as much standing space as authorities or passengers will tolerate. Standing/sitting ratios of 3:1 are not uncommon but may exceed 5:1. Double deck buses are far less common - large fleets are found mainly in India and Indonesia. The use of large articulated buses is rare, except in major Chinese cities where large fleets of articulated buses and trolley buses are found. (Articulated buses and trolleybuses are reviewed in more detail in Chapter 3).

Bus designs provide capacities which range from 12 passengers in minibuses to over 170 in large double-deck buses (Table 2.1). However, generally design capacity has little meaning in Third World cities. During peak periods buses frequently carry as many passengers as can squeeze in or hang onto them. Over 240 passengers have been observed on individual articulated buses in Dar Es Salaam, and this is probably by no means a record.

TABLE 2.1
Capacity of Urban Buses

Type of bus	Design Capacity		Typical peak period crush loading
	Seated	Total	
Minibus	12	20	40
Small bus	20	30	50
Adapted truck	20	35	45
Medium bus (standard bus)	40	80	105
Large single-deck bus	50	100	125
Double deck-bus	80	120	150
Large double-deck bus	80	170	200
Articulated bus	55	120	150
Large articulated bus	55	170	210

Source: World Bank Studies

4

Plate 2.1a   A privately operated standard bus, being used under contract to Delhi Transport Corporation

Plate 2.1b   A short wheel-base bus, particularly suited to the hilly terrain of Medellin, Colombia

Plate 2.1c   An unusual high-capacity tractor-trailer unit, developed in India

Plate 2.1d   An example of Ghana's famous 'Mammy Wagons'

Plate 2.2   Monrovia: the influence of street trading on traffic

With crush conditions the norm in most developing countries, it is not unusual to find bus passenger volumes approaching the volumes experienced on metros in industrial countries. Bus systems operating in mixed traffic regularly carry up to 15,000 passengers per hour in one lane. Where more than one lane of mixed traffic is available, volumes of 20,000 passengers per hour, and more, have been achieved, (eg.Pusan, Hong Kong, Lagos, Bogota etc). When buses are given some form of priority, such as bus only lanes or exclusive busways, even higher volumes in a single lane are evident. (Busways are discussed in Chapter 5 "Busway Transit". Other bus priority schemes are discussed in Chapter 9 "Traffic Management"). In many cases high passenger volumes occur when the route involves a mixture of large and small buses and minibuses. The two southbound lanes of the Carter Bridge in Lagos together carry in excess of 40,000 passengers in a mixture of medium size buses and minibuses during the peak hour. In a single reserved lane in Bangkok, 250 standard buses and 150 minibuses an hour carry more than 18,000 passengers during the peak. What minibuses lack in passenger capacity, they often make up for in speed and manoeuvrability, which is a considerable asset in narrow congested streets.

Most urban roads that carry heavy passenger volumes generally have provision for 2 traffic lanes, and in some cases 3 traffic lanes, in each direction. Under these circumstances, with adequate traffic management, buses achieve journey speeds of between 15 to 20 kmph or more.

In all but the very largest cities, even on the highest demand corridors during peak periods, passenger volumes are usually well within the possible limit for buses and minibuses. As would be expected, volumes are comparatively low throughout the remainder of the network and during the off peak. Nevertheless, during peak periods services can be seriously disrupted, particularly along the main commuter routes, because of traffic congestion, parking and street trading activities (Plate 2.2). There is often the opportunity to spread the peak load from busy routes onto other roads serving the same corridor and to provide alternative and possibly more attractive routes for passengers who do not need to pass though high demand and congested areas. However, the tendency is often the reverse, with operators concentrating in congested areas to maximise patronage as in the case of jeepneys in Manila and minibuses in Karachi. In some cities this has been avoided by effective traffic management and control, and more rational fare and route regulations.

Bus and minibus services are found to display considerable flexibility in meeting changes in the pattern of city development and levels of demand. This flexibility is of particular value in developing cities which are experiencing rapid growth and significant land use changes. However, in some cities flexibility is inhibited by undue regulations and slow government response to changes. Where they are not unduly bound by regulation, bus operators are found to provide a reasonable level of service and to be cost effective along both low and high demand routes. Since they often fan out into low density areas, much inconvenient and time consuming interchanging between services is avoided.

Despite the vital role that buses are able to play, services are frequently insufficient to meet demand, and the services that are provided suffer from low output and are often inconvenient, uncomfortable and unsafe. Certainly many bus operators are hard pressed to meet the basic quality of service indicators devised by the World Bank (see Table 2.2).

Journey times, in particular, frequently fall below reasonable standards. For example, in Mexico City a third of all commuters spend between two and four hours each day travelling to and from work. In Cairo bus journey speeds are between 3 and 13kmph. In Bogota journey speeds for buses average 25 to 30kmph but drop to 7kmph in the central area. Similarly waiting times are often excessive with the average well above the recommended maximum. Delhi is fairly typical with average waiting times on a number of routes well above 20 minutes. Nevertheless in some cities bus operators are able to achieve, and in some cases exceed basic standards (e.g. Hong Kong, Buenos Aires, Coimbatore and Seoul).

The quantity and quality of services provided by both public and private sector operators are often below requirements for a number of reasons:-

- traffic congestion and unkept or poorly paved roads cause slow journey speeds and breakdowns, leading to low output and high operating costs;
- a lack of investment in vehicles and spares due to the imposition of low fares and restricted access to funds, in particular foreign exchange;
- inappropriate government regulation of routes and restrictions in the choice of vehicles.

Under these circumstances it is not uncommon to find both the public and private sectors struggling to meet the demand for bus services: the situation in Karachi, for example, is fairly typical of that in many Third World cities (Box 2.1).

Bus services have in the past been dominated by public sector operations, and currently most cities continue to have one or sometimes two or more publicly owned bus corporations. However they have suffered declining effectiveness and viability and have been quite unable to cope with the very rapidly growing demands of recent years. In most cities the gap has been readily filled by private operators who now command by far the greater share of the market despite often facing

TABLE 2.2
Quality of service indicators

1. *Waiting time*
    Passenger waiting time at bus stops
        Average   5-10 minutes
        Maximum   10-20 minutes

2. *Walking distance to bus stops*
    Dense urban areas   300-500 m
    Low-density urban areas   500-1000 m

3. *Interchanges between routes and services*
    The number of times a passenger has to
    change buses or other modes on a journey
    to or from work:
        Average   0-1
        Maximum   (less than 10% of commuters)   2

4. *Journey times*
    Hours travelling each day to *and* from work:
        Average   1.0-1.5
        Maximum   2-3

    Journey speeds of buses:
    Dense areas in mixed traffic   10-12kmph
    Bus-only lanes   15-18kmph
    Low-density areas   25 kmph

5. *Travel expenditure*
    Household expenditure on travel as
    a percentage of household income   10

Source: World Bank Technical Paper 68, 'Bus services: reducing costs, raising standards'

serious difficulties. Studies by the World Bank indicate that the private sector accounts for more that 75 per cent of all bus trips in the Third World, and practically all paratransit trips. While by contrast, public bus corporations continue to be prominent in China and India, even in these countries the emergence of private operators is becoming increasingly evident (Table 2.3).

The increasing share of the market captured by private operators has arisen mainly because of growth in demand and their ability to remain viable. In particular, in the interests of survival, private operators have strong motives to keep costs down, and do this by reducing waste and overheads and in particular by employing the minimum of staff. By contrast, with much of their revenue coming from subsidies, public bus corporations have little incentive to keep costs down. Also they are invariably saddled with very large work forces which often cannot be reduced for political reasons. As a result, the costs of public corporations generally are roughly double those of the private sector bus operators operating on the same routes and under the same conditions. Even where the same low fares are charged, private operators are able to make modest profits while the public corporations often make substantial losses.

The substantial differences in staffing ratios, understandably, has a marked impact on the cost

KARACHI PUBLIC TRANSPORT BOX 2.1

As in many Third World cities, massive increases in demand for transport in Karachi have not been matched by sufficient investment in transport infrastructure and services. As a result, public transport conditions in Karachi have seriously deteriorated and have been aggravated by a consequent swing towards the extensive use of private cars. To overcome this unsatisfactory situation the Government plans to introduce a mass transit system comprising busways and possibly LRT.

Currently public transport services in Karachi are provided by some 450 large public sector buses (Karachi Transport Corporation: KTC), and a very large number of private sector vehicles including 1000 medium buses, 2000 large minibuses, 1000 small minibuses, 6000 taxis and 10000 auto rickshaws. There are also about 1000 school buses and buses run by companies for their employees. A very small number of commuter trains are run by the Pakistan Railway on its circular and suburban branch lines. Private sector buses and minibuses carry more than 95 per cent of all public transport trips in Karachi. Most buses are heavily utilized and over-loaded and it has been estimated that there is a short fall of almost 2000 buses and minibuses.

Bus fares are set by the provincial Government. While increases have been made recently, these are not sufficient to encourage badly needed investment. Currently fares are less than half those found in most other large Third World cities.

Due to an excessively large work force of about 4000, substantial revenue leakage and management problems, KTC operates at very substantial losses estimated at US$6 million per year. Also, with very low productivity, KTC has very little impact in meeting the needs of the city.

Most private bus services are small enterprises comprising only one or two buses, often operated by owner-drivers. Generally they are very cost effective. However, poor returns due to restraints on fares and little access to foreign exchange have discouraged investment in expansion, replacement vehicles or spares. This, together with restrictions on the number of minibuses, has lead to a significant reduction in the size and quality of the bus fleet in recent years.

There are about 5,500 taxis and 10,000 auto-rickshaws in regular service in Karachi. They are very popular with mid-income groups and account for 15 per cent of fare paying trips in Karachi. Fares are ten times as high as bus fares, providing a clear indication that many passengers are prepared to pay more for more convenient services.

structures of public and private operators. In the case of public corporations, staff costs account for about a third of their total costs but may exceed 50 per cent as for example at the Ankara bus corporation (55 per cent). For private operators staff costs are generally in the region of 10 per cent of total cost but may be as high as 30 per cent where labour costs are rising. However records are not very reliable, because of methods of payment, including profit sharing.

An example of the comparative performance and cost structures of public and private bus operators is presented in Tables 2.4 and 2.5. The results of a comprehensive survey by The Central Institute of Road Transport (Pune) of costs of some 55 Indian State bus undertakings are summarised in Table 2.6.

In a number of countries a degree of deregulation has greatly stimulated the private sector. For example, the easing of import restrictions in Sri Lanka led to the import of over 6000 buses by

TABLE 2.3
Bus services: characteristics and costs
Private and public bus services operating in the same city. (1985 data)

City	Ownership	Type of Buses	Fleet	Fleet Utilization	Staff/Bus Ratio	Fare for 5 Km US$	Cost Pass/Km UScents	Revenue Cost Ratio
Accra	Public	Large SD	44	24	28.2	0.13(G)	-	0.51
	Private	Regular SD	665	73	5.5	0.18G)	-	1.40
Ankara	Public	Large SD	900	65	6.0	0.12(F)	2.5	0.67
	Private	Large SD	200	95	2.6	0.12(F)	1.2	1.70
Bangkok	Public	Large SD	4,400	80	6.2	0.07(F)	1.9	0.74
	Private	Large SD	550	80	-	0.07(F)	1.2	1.10
	Private	Mini	12,000	-	-	0.07(F)	-	1.20
Calcutta	Public	Large SD, DD	1,100	64	20.7	0.04(G)	1.9	0.46
	Private	Large SD	2,200	86	4.0	0.04(G)	0.7	1.10
	Private	Small SD	950	88	3.8	0.08(G)	1.0	1.35
Istanbul	Public	Large SD, Art	1,500	60	7.5	0.14(F)	2.0	0.88
	Private	Large SD	960	-	-	0.14(F)	1.7	1.10
	Private	Mini	3,800	78	-	0.20(G)	2.2	1.40
Jakarta	Public	Large SD, DD	1,940	59	14.5	0.13(F)	1.8	0.50
	Private	Large SD	550	76	7.25	0.13(F)	0.9	1.20
	Private	Mini	3,365	80	5.5	0.13(F)	1.2	1.45
Karachi	Public	Large SD	790	40	12.4	0.04(F)	2.8	0.49
	Private	Regular SD	1,320	72	6.4	0.04(F)	1.0	1.15
	Private	Mini	3,980	80	5.7	0.06(F)	1.3	1.30
Khartoum	Public	Large SD	74	65	18.1	0.08(G)	1.5	0.80
	Public/ Military	Large SD	141	78	8.0	0.08(G)	0.7	1.00
	Private	Converted trucks	720	80	4.5	0.06(G)	0.6	1.10
Mexico City	Public	Large SD	6,500	87	5.7	0.01(F)	1.6	0.12
	Private	Large SD	9,000	-	-	0.09(F)	-	1.00
Sao Paulo	Public	Large SD/Art	3,280	82	7.6	0.26(F)	-	-
	Private	Large SD	5,850	90	5.1	0.26(F)	-	-

"Staff/Bus Ratio" is in respect of operating buses

SD = Single Deck Buses F = Flat Fare
DD = Double Deck Buses G = Graduated Fares (ie., related to distance)
Art = Articulated Buses

Source: World Bank surveys and studies

TABLE 2.4
Performance of public and private bus operators

Bus operator performance indicators (ranges)

	Public	*Private*
Average fleet availability (%)	47-85	80-89
Passengers per bus daily	1200-2200	200-2900
Passengers per km operated	7.6-10.1	1.2-12.1
Daily km per bus operated	160-220	170-240
Staff per bus operated	5.8-13.5	1.0-3.7
Load factor	0.3-0.6	0.6-0.9
Profitability (revenue: cost)	0.6-1.2	0.9-3.6

Source: TRL Research Report 294

TABLE 2.5
Public and private bus operators

Cost structures (percentages)

	Public operator			*Private operator*		
	Douala	*Yaounde*	*Dar es Salaam*	*Harare*	*Dar es Salaam*	*Jos*
Staff/personnel	40.0	26.8	29.3	23.0	11.0	6.5
Fuel/lubricants	13.5	11.6	19.4	22.5	31.7	31.5
Tyres, tubes, spares & maintenance	15.0	14.8	16.3	40.8	23.9	18.5
Depreciation/interest	20.2	24.1	9.0	5.8	28.8	42.5
Taxes/licence/insurance	4.3	3.0	1.2	0.7	4.6	1.0
Miscellaneous	7.0	19.7	24.8	7.2	-	-

Source: TRL Research Report 294

TABLE 2.6
Indian state transport undertakings: cost structure

Factor	*Cost structure (percentages)*
Personnel	33
Fuel and lubricants	20
Tyres, tubes and spares	13
Depreciation	22
Taxes	12
Total	100

Source: Central Institute of Road Transport, Pune

private operators. This resulted in a significant and immediate increase in overall capacity of the public transport system, with more frequent and less crowded bus services. In other places a lack of regulation and enforcement has led to the concentration of very many buses and minibuses in central areas, causing substantial congestion. In Manila, for example, congestion caused by minibuses has reduced some of the expected benefits of the light rail system (Box 7.2). Similar congestion and disruption is caused by minibuses in Jakarta and Santiago.

PRIVATE SECTOR BUS SERVICES

Private sector bus and minibus operations have grown significantly in Third World conurbations and make a considerable contribution to the supply of bus services. They use a wide variety of vehicles and, although working under difficult conditions, they seem able to achieve reasonable levels of service and are generally profitable.

Most private bus services are small enterprises or family businesses comprising only one or two buses, either owner-operated or leased on a daily or weekly basis. In some cities operators have formed themselves into cooperatives or route associations but often retain a high degree of independence and self sufficiency.

Apart from low staffing levels, private operators are able to achieve some degree of viability by keeping down overheads. For example, rather than using specially constructed depots, vehicles are often parked overnight within owners' plots, on-street or on spare ground. They are maintained by the crews themselves, by family members or mechanics shared with other operators.

One of the most significant reasons why private operators are financially viable is the low level of revenue leakage (fare evasion by passengers and pilferage of collected fares by crews and other staff). In the case of owner-drivers or small family run businesses, revenue leakage is practically non-existent. Other types of privately owned enterprises reduce revenue leakage in a number of ways. For example, they may hire out their buses for fixed amounts or may require their crews to hand in a predetermined amount each day. In either case, the crews retain any surplus revenue as their remuneration. The amount due to the owner is readily adjusted to reflect increased costs, improved overall revenue, and variations between routes, so that both the owners and crews obtain a reasonable return.

Large private operators are generally the exception in Third World cities, mainly because they are inclined to suffer from some of the problems of the public corporations such as revenue leakage. However, despite the difficulties, a few have achieved good results. Examples of these are the Kenya Bus Services in Nairobi and the King of Kings Bus Company in Accra. One of the largest and most successful private operators in the world is The Kowloon Motor Bus Company in Hong Kong with a fleet of nearly 3000 large buses. All three companies exercise close control of cost and revenue collection, and have strong and effective management.

In only a few countries is the provision of bus services completely unrestricted. In many places regulations exist to control the introduction of additional buses or bus routes, but because of overwhelming demand, these are often ignored or relaxed. Where there is only moderate regulation, services are generally found to more closely meet the needs of the public. But in many places the process of increasing the supply of buses is inhibited or discouraged by slow or obstructive government procedures. The involvement of unions in some cases has the same effect and results in restrictive or undesirable monopolistic practices. In some cities, Rio de Janeiro and Accra for example, unions are given the authority to allocate routes on the basis of demand. Under these circumstances unions, more concerned with the interests of their members, may tend to suppress competition. But in most countries private sector bus services are both very responsive to demands and cost effective: a combination which is inevitably favourable to the public, as in the case of the 10 million passengers using private sector buses in Buenos Aires (Box 2.2).

BUENOS AIRES: PRIVATE SECTOR BUS SERVICES   BOX 2.2

Commuters in Buenos Aires benefit from a most effective and well organised private sector public transport system. This comprises a fleet of 15,000 privately owned buses, known as "colectivos", which account for 83 per cent of public transport trips. Metro and suburban rail systems and taxis share the remainder. No publicly owned buses have been in operation since 1955, when an unprofitable publicly owned system was dissolved. Most buses are locally manufactured 21-seaters with a total capacity of 60 passengers. Despite their comparative small size, each bus on average carries between 850 to 1,100 passengers per day. All buses are one-man-operated and are able to operate at a profit while providing a range of good services to passengers. Their total patronage has been estimated at 10 million passengers each day.

The fleet is organized into 300 route associations called "empresas" that represent individual owners or small groups of partners in ownership. The owners are responsible for operating and maintaining their vehicles, while each empresa assumes responsibility for scheduling bus services. They provide their members with administrative and legal services and generally function as operators unions. Since fares are fixed by the government an important role of empresas is to negotiate fare increases on behalf of their members.

In most cases, the owners keep the fares collected but the empresa ensures equitable earnings by interchanging routes and schedules on a weekly basis. The system is one in which operating cost risks are borne by the owner, while revenue risks are shared between the owner and the empresa.

Despite close cooperation, operators compete vigorously and since fares are fixed they vie for passengers by emphasising quality, speed and frequency.

Most private operators favour buses based on production-line chassis with locally fabricated bodies. These generally are substantially cheaper to purchase and maintain than limited-production or custom-built buses.

While there are many examples of operators choosing large buses that have proven to be cost-effective, their inclination is generally towards the smaller vehicles. Even in a city where small vehicles are banned from the city centre, for example Mexico City and Istanbul, large numbers of small buses and paratransit vehicles often proliferate throughout the remainder of the city. Apart from better utilization, smaller capital outlay, and ease of maintenance, the tendency towards small vehicles stems from a number of other factors, for example:

(a)   drivers of small buses often have to meet less stringent requirements for driving permits than do drivers of large buses and thus can be paid less. Inspection requirements for small buses may also be less costly than for large buses;

(b)   although small buses result in a higher ratio of drivers to passengers, this is not a significant disadvantage in most developing countries where labour costs are low;

(c)   fares are easier to collect on small buses than on large buses, and the chances of revenue leakage are much reduced;

(d)   small buses are easier to manoeuvre and are quicker in congested traffic conditions. In some cities minibuses are the only form of public transport able to negotiate the labyrinth of narrow streets.

Maintenance of private buses is often carried out by drivers with some assistance from crews, family members or mechanics shared with other operators, hence the preference for vehicles which require only basic skills for maintenance. The need for more extensive or complex maintenance (such as calibration of fuel injectors) may be put to manufacturers local agents, but more often than not is undertaken by back street garages. Maintenance difficulties are one of the reasons why private operators shy away from larger buses, especially those that are custom built. These often involve sophisticated and non-standard equipment (for example, retarders, articulation systems, remote control doors, relay circuitry etc.). As a result, maintenance of large buses tends to require specially trained staff and special facilities, adding considerably to the costs, or, if neglected, to frequent breakdowns.

A major factor in the cost of maintenance and bus out-turn is the spare parts situation which in turn has a strong influence on the choice of vehicles. Often the chassis and engine components of popular production-line vehicles are common to a wide variety of models, so that spares for trucks, vans and cars can be used for the maintenance of buses and minibuses. Such spares generally are more readily available and cheaper than those required for less common or custom built vehicles. Nevertheless, in many countries import restrictions and a lack of funds and foreign exchange cause a serious shortage of even commonly used spare parts, leading to many buses and minibuses being off the road for long periods.

A characteristic of private sector operators in the Third World has been their tireless efforts, and very considerable resourcefulness and ingenuity in overcoming their difficulties. In particular, despite the lack of proper equipment, materials and replacements, they are able to keep vehicles running. Technology has been developed to rehabilitate unserviceable and even scrapped vehicles, adapting and fabricating make-shift parts, and constructing body work by hand. With very little going to waste, they put to shame the meagre recycling efforts of industrialised countries. The standard of rehabilitation is generally very high and the cost of rehabilitated buses is barely a quarter of the cost of new ones. There is certainly no shortage of buses suitable for rehabilitation and in most cities there is no shortage of enterprises doing this sort of work.

In many places operators make remarkable efforts to overcome their problems and also display considerable pride, as is evident from the very elaborate and painstaking decoration of vehicles (Plate 2.3).

Plate 2.3   Well-decorated private bus: Karachi

COOPERATION BETWEEN OPERATORS

Cooperation among private operators is common throughout the developing countries. In many places it has resulted in the provision of more cost-effective and reliable services, benefiting both the operators and the travelling public. Cooperation is usually effected through route associations, operators' unions, or cooperatives. In addition to providing miscellaneous services, the organizations often exercise a degree of supervision and control that provides an effective compromise between a complete free-for-all at one extreme, and undue government regulation at the other. In this way, the disruptive and dangerous practices often attributed to free market conditions are lessened. Generally competition is retained. In the case of the route associations (empresas) in Buenos Aires competition is fierce with emphasis on frequency and quality of service (See Box 2.2). However, in some cases cooperation has led to restrictive practices and price fixing. For example, in Santiago, where there is little government regulation, the route associations have formed cartels and set high fares: they deter new operators and expansion and take strong action against any undercutting of fares.

The services provided by operators' associations to their members often include: a forum for discussing fares, routes, facilities, and policy issues with public authorities; negotiating contracts and wages with labour unions; the management of terminals and the dispatching of vehicles; the purchase of vehicles and spares; the provision of servicing and maintenance facilities; common

16

insurance, legal advice, and assistance; and the training of drivers and mechanics. The degree of support varies very considerably. For example, a full range of services on the above lines is provided to members by cooperatives in Montevideo, while in the case of minibus associations in Jakarta, services are limited to the control of terminals with a degree of coercion.

In several cities route associations allocate bus routes and schedule services, and they may collect and share out revenue. This function is undertaken in order to overcome the problem of providing services on routes that are commercially unattractive but which nonetheless need to be served. The aim is a more equitable distribution of income among operators so that those providing a less rewarding but valuable service to the public are not penalized. In Daejeon, Korea, the bus cooperative achieves this aim by an elaborate system in which the city is divided into four zones, with each served by a group of different bus companies. The groups are rotated between zones weekly so that every company has a turn of profitable and unprofitable routes. A similar arrangement is equally successful in Incheon, Korea.

PUBLIC SECTOR BUS SERVICES

Most cities have at least one publicly owned bus corporation or company. Typically they operate large fleets comprising 500 to 2500 medium to large capacity buses. Particularly large fleets of buses in public ownership are found in Latin America (Mexico City: 6500; Sao Paulo: 3300), China (Shanghai:5000; Beijing:4500)and India (Delhi:4200; Bombay:2500). Much smaller fleets of up to 500 buses are common in many African cities.

Public ownership may be in the hands of central government or city governments. Frequently chief executives and senior managers are government officials. The work force, including drivers, also are usually civil servants on civil service pay scales and terms of employment. Few public bus corporations are completely autonomous, but in some places there is a growing trend towards commercial practices with powers to hire and fire staff. However, even these semi-autonomous corporations often face personnel difficulties because of the influence of unions. As they are usually funded by government, freedom to make important policy decisions, particularly with regard to financial issues, is strictly limited. Some notable exceptions are found in India where one of the most successful public bus corporations is the Cheran Transport Corporation (CTC) located in Coimbatore (Box 2.3).

Often public bus corporations hold very considerable assets in the form of buildings and land as well as equipment and rolling stock. However, in relation to the total needs of cities, the magnitude of public sector bus services is usually quite small and insignificant compared to the private sector. Nevertheless, because public corporation buses and terminals usually have a distinctive livery and high profile, particularly in city centres, they often give a false impression of extensive operations.

With very few exceptions public bus corporations are subsidised, many quite heavily. These subsidies arise generally because on the one hand costs are excessive, and on the other, productivity and revenue are very low. (See Box 2.4: Jakarta Public Bus Corporation (PPD))

COIMBATORE, INDIA: PUBLIC BUS CORPORATION BOX 2.3

The Cheran Transport Corporation (CTC), in Coimbatore, India, is a very rare example of a profitable public bus corporation. It was created in 1972 when the state government nationalized all private transport enterprises with more than 100 vehicles. CTC was mandated by the state to provide cheap and efficient bus services while maintaining financial viability. The new company's directors maintained the corporate structure and practice already in place and have concentrated on improving efficiency and development. As a result, CTC has been able to generate a substantial operating surplus while providing good service to its passengers. Beginning with 300 buses in 1972, the company now operates 1,086 buses that each carry about 1,100 passengers daily. CTC operates in competition with 520 private buses at the same fares. The company employs 7.3 staff members per operating bus which is a little better than most public corporations. However, its fleet utilization rate at 95 per cent is exceptionally high.

Fares are set by the state government, which otherwise has little involvement with the company. CTC, for example, can borrow from any source and the board of directors is free to appoint managers based exclusively on professional criteria. It is organized into several branches, or depots, according to a highly decentralized pattern in which branch managers have total responsibility for operations, maintenance and finance. Staff receive a salary and a small percentage of daily receipts. The salary structure reflects seniority and performance; bonuses are awarded on the basis of achievement. The accounting system is computerized, reducing the need for more clerical personnel, and to further reduce the staff to bus ratio, there is a gradual switch to one-man bus operation.

The company has its own body building operation, with a target of 750 bodies per annum. More than half of the bodies manufactured are sold to other bus companies, generating substantial revenue.

As a result of these practices, CTC earns a net profit in the region of US$750,000 per year. The operating ratio of total revenue over costs, excluding interest, is about 1.05. After distributing 25 per cent of the surplus among employees and paying state surtaxes of 16 per cent, the company transfers the remainder to a general reserve fund to be reinvested in fleet expansion.

The success of CTC sends a clear message of the importance of minimal government interference and of management and staff motivation through incentives.

One of the primary reasons for the high cost of publicly owned services is that, as noted earlier, they are frequently overstaffed. It is not uncommon to find public bus corporations with staffing ratios (staff per operating bus) in excess of eight, and very often between 10 and 15 or even higher (eg. Lagos 13; Jakarta 14; Calcutta 20 and Accra 28). On the other hand, private operations have staffing ratios of about five, or even as low as two or three in the case of owner-drivers or small family enterprises.

The high staffing ratios of public corporations often arise because redundant staff cannot be laid off or retired, due either to government regulations or union influence. This is a particularly intractable problem with the Karachi Transport Corporation which has over 500 redundant staff and many others under-employed. Even though wages are generally low, the sheer magnitude of overstaffing can be a cause of very considerable losses. Also, public corporations often have excessive layers of management and use elaborate administrative procedures employing large clerical and accounting staffs. Such arrangements add considerably to overheads and may impair, rather than enhance, productivity.

18

With a few notable exceptions (mainly in India) public bus corporations are rarely able to out-shed more than 60-70 per cent of their bus fleets in peak periods. In addition, the number of public buses in service is often substantially reduced as the day progresses because of a high rate of breakdowns. In Calcutta almost a third (200) of the corporation buses which start out in the morning have broken down by the end of the day.

When compared to private buses, the lower proportion of public buses in service can be attributed to a lack of incentives, a high level of absenteeism, poor maintenance, and a shortage of spares. Clearly, buses that are out of service represent a substantial loss of earnings and a waste of capital resources. With much higher staffing ratios, staff productivity is naturally much lower in public corporations than in private enterprises. Measured in terms of passenger-kilometres per staff member per day, staff productivity for the average public corporation, at 500-600, is roughly half that of private enterprises at 1,100-1,300.

Many public corporations are plagued by a loss of revenue due to: fare evasion by passengers (hanging onto the outside of buses for this purpose is popular in some cities); bus crews being tardy in the collection of fares; and fares collected being stolen by bus crews or other staff. Revenue losses of 10-15 per cent are not uncommon and may be as high as 30 per cent in some cases. But even at comparatively small levels, revenue leakage can spell the difference between making a profit and incurring a loss. The issuing of tickets or tokens and the use of secure fare boxes and turnstiles, are designed to overcome these losses, and have a measure of success. But where there is collusion between passengers, collectors and inspectors, even sophisticated systems are far from being completely secure.

Some corporations attempt to limit revenue loss by requiring their crews to hand in a predetermined amount each day, allowing or turning a blind eye to crews retaining any surplus. However, the public sector corporations, when faced with rising costs, generally are unable to overcome the considerable resistance of crews to the adjustment of the basic amount they have to hand in. Because of this, in a number of cases, corporations have been running at a considerable loss, while crews with union protection are receiving excessive rewards. Karachi's KTC (Box.2.1) and Jakarta's PPD (Box 2.4) are examples of this situation, and like most public bus corporations have to be heavily subsidised.

A number of public bus corporations, given a degree of freedom to make changes, have effectively reduced costs and improved efficiency by adopting commercial practices and hiving off some of their work or responsibilities. For example, the public bus corporation responsible for bus services in Istanbul has found most routes to be unprofitable. To overcome substantial losses and because of its inability to meet growing demands, the corporation employs private operators on contract to meet a large part of its commitments. Not only do the private operators make a profit on these "unprofitable" routes at the same fares charged on the corporation buses, but they also pay 10 per cent of their revenue to the corporation. Variations of these arrangements are employed successfully in other cities with the private operators contracted to run bus routes using either corporation buses or their own buses. Under these contracts the private operators are required to meet specified performance levels which are monitored by government or corporation inspectors.

Some public sector corporations lease their buses to private operators, but unlike the contract system, the private operators are free to operate routes of their own choice and to determine the

JAKARTA PUBLIC BUS CORPORATION **BOX 2.4**

The Penang Kutan Penumpang Djakarta (PPD) displays most of the deficiencies shown by publicly owned bus corporations. It operates in the Jakarta metropolitan region, which has a population of about 16 million. The city sprawls over a large amount of territory with no defined city centre; business and housing development occurs along main roads, and small communities (kampungs) are squeezed in between. An estimated 40 per cent of the road network is operating under unacceptably congested conditions.

In addition to PPD, the private sector operates a wide variety of vehicles, including single-deckers, minibuses and microbuses. Only one private firm, Mayasari Bakti, is licensed to operate conventional single-decker buses. The municipal agency responsible for transportation regulates licensing, fares, frequencies and routes, and is supposed to evaluate whether existing patterns satisfy demand. Lack of staff and funds has meant that, in practice, there is little regulation or coordination.

PPD owns over 2,300 conventional double and single-deck buses, and employs over 16,500 people. It carries about 2 million passengers daily. But neither productivity levels, nor the quality of its service is satisfactory. Operating costs are particularly high in relation to output. Only about 60 per cent of its buses are in operation every day. This poor turnout is partly due to its fleet (especially the double-deckers) being overly sophisticated given the difficult operating conditions and the lack of facilities and trained maintenance personnel. Long passenger queues, overcrowding and unreliable frequency all characterize the PPD bus routes.

The fare system is based on a flat rate, which allows many passengers to travel up to 25 kilometres for less than US 20 cents, while others must purchase transfers for far shorter trips. Drivers and conductors turn over a predetermined portion of the total revenue collected to PPD and divide the rest among themselves. Although the system has some advantages (for example, it provides an incentive to maximize fare collection), they are outweighed by its disadvantages: drivers add to congestion by stopping in unauthorized places to pick up passengers, layover times at terminals are lengthened as drivers wait for more passengers and PPD loses a substantial amount of revenue because unions have successfully prevented the company from raising its share of income. PPD covers only 50 per cent of its full costs and 76 per cent of operating costs; it incurs losses of about US$30 million each year.

As a result of its ongoing losses, PPD has not been able to keep up with the city's growing demand for public transport and the private sector is serving about 60-65 per cent of the market. The private companies charge the same fares as PPD but because their costs are roughly half those of PPD they are able to make a profit while PPD needs massive subsidies.

level of service. Coupled with competition, the advantage of this arrangement is that operators more readily respond to the needs of the public. Safeguards are included to ensure that the buses receive proper maintenance and attention.

3 ARTICULATED BUSES AND TROLLEYBUSES.

A comparatively small number of cities have introduced articulated buses and trolleybuses into their public transport systems. Generally these are in the public sector, with a few exceptions in South America (Plate 3.1).

Plate 3.1   Articulated bus, Porto Alegre, Brazil

ARTICULATED BUSES

The largest fleets of articulated buses are found in China notably Beijing and Shanghai. Outside China fleets are much smaller, generally less than 100 except for Istanbul, Tunis and Cairo. (See Table 3.1) The higher capacity and potential high revenue earnings of articulated buses may be attractive, but cost effectiveness is often impaired by high operating and capital costs. In Dar es Salaam both conventional buses and articulated buses are used by the same bus company. While the conventional buses make a profit, the articulated buses, which are being phased out, sustain a substantial loss. Maintenance problems and costs can be aggravated by uneven road surfaces which can cause serious damage to the costly articulation mechanisms. The high cost and level of technology, including the expected long term involvement of expatriate technicians, are seen as distinct drawbacks. For example, for these reasons serious doubts are being expressed by authorities in Addis Ababa and Nairobi about proposals to introduce articulated buses into their cities. On the other hand, the large fleets of articulated buses in China have not presented any

TABLE 3.1
Articulated bus and trolleybus fleets

Cities with large fleets	Fleet size
Articulated buses	
Beijing	2500
Shanghai	3700
Tianjin	1500
(Approx 20 other Chinese cities)	(100 - 500)
Istanbul	370
Tunis	175
Cairo	150
Trolley buses	
Shanghai	1000
Beijing	550
(Approx 20 other Chinese cities)	(100 - 500)
Mexico City	800
Sao Paulo	480
Bogota	400
Pyongyang	400

Source: Jane's Urban Transport Systems 1991 and author's research

particular maintenance or operational problems. This is principally because they are manufactured locally to designs which have been developed over many years and which fully take into account local conditions and technology. Also valuable maintenance advice and assistance is readily available from the manufacturers, usually located in the same city. The role played by The Bus and Coach Plant Corporation in Shanghai is a good example of the value of local experience and involvement of manufacturers. (See Box 3.1)

TROLLEYBUSES

Trolleybuses are comparatively rare in Third World cities and where they do exist they are usually in small fleets of less than 100. The exceptions are the large fleets of trolleybuses found in Shanghai, Mexico City, Beijing and Sao Paulo (Plate 3.2). Even in these cities, trolleybuses form only a small part of the public transport system. Although trolleybuses provide capacity similar to that of large conventional buses and are environmentally attractive, costs are high, particularly for the power transmission systems. In line with the experience of other electric transport systems, the high investment in trolleybuses cannot generally be justified on the basis of combustible fuel savings or other economic benefits. Trolleybuses are also tied to their power transmission systems and are at a distinct disadvantage where the development process frequently necessitates rerouting because of changes in demand, road works, and traffic management. Thus they lack the considerable advantage of flexibility provided by buses. For example, a major part of the trolleybus system in Izmir, Turkey, was put out of action for several months during the laying of a water main in a road close to the depot. At other times power failures

SHANGHAI ARTICULATED BUSES AND TROLLEYBUSES   BOX 3.1

The Shanghai Transit Corporation operates the largest public transport system in China and by far the largest fleet of articulated buses and articulated trolleybuses anywhere in the world. Daily average ridership is in the region of 15 million and on occasions tops 17 million. The corporation, which is a state enterprise, is heavily subsidised by the municipality :fare revenue covers only 50 per cent of costs.

The fleet comprises 5000 large buses and 1000 trolleybuses. Of these, 3700 buses and all of the trolleybuses are articulated. All the vehicles are manufactured locally by the Shanghai Bus and Coach Plant following traditional designs developed over many years of experience with the conditions found in Shanghai. Almost all the buses are petrol driven but there is a move towards diesel engines. More than half of the trolleybuses are thyristor chopper controlled.

Typical of the articulated buses recently put into service is the SK662KP. This has an overall length of 14.6 meters and is designed primarily as a "standee bus" with seating for 23 passengers and a rated maximum total capacity of 155. Crush loading is in the region of 180 passengers. The average number of passengers carried daily by each articulated bus is in excess of 2300.

While articulated trolleybuses are slightly smaller in size and rated capacity, they serve the highest demand routes in the centre of the city and achieve massive utilization: each carries on average as many as 4500 passengers per day. Articulated trolleybuses recently put into service include the SK561G.

With slow moving bicycles forming a high proportion of vehicular traffic and with very high pedestrian movements, roads in central Shanghai are heavily congested. As a result, buses and trolleybuses which run almost nose to tail during rush hours, are often unable to exceed journey speeds of 10kmph in the city centre. Journey speed are a little better outside the centre and are as much as 25kmph in the suburbs.

Although subject to constant excessive loading and demanding traffic conditions, buses and trolleybuses in Shanghai perform well. Unlike services under similar circumstances in other countries, breakdowns are very infrequent and daily out-shedding is as high as 96 per cent. Much of the credit for this is attributed to the suitability of the vehicles. Designs and development are based on much experience of operating under the actual road and traffic conditions in Shanghai and knowledge of the level of local skills. Also, replacements and spares are readily available from the manufacturer based in the city.

and breakdowns have put large sections of the system out of operation. Dual mode trolleybuses that are able to convert to diesel operation are available to provide greater flexibility and to overcome power failures, but these are more than double the cost of conventional buses.

Generally, as well as much higher capital costs, the maintenance of trolleybuses and their power distribution systems require skills that are not readily available in most cities. As a result most trolleybus systems require heavy subsidies and are almost always owned by public corporations. One of the most technically successful systems is the trolleybus busway along the Avenida 9 de Julho in Sao Paulo. But despite very high usage and local skills well able to cope with the level of technology involved, the system requires heavy capital and operating subsidies. The system, including the busway, power transmission, depots and terminals has required a capital grant equivalent to US$15 million per km. Far from being able to make a contribution to capital costs the fare box revenue is only able to cover 40 per cent of operating costs. The Mexico City

Plate 3.2   Fleet of new trolley buses, Sao Paulo, Brazil

trolleybus system fares even worse, and although heavily utilised, the revenue covers less than 10 per cent of operating costs. Clearly trolleybus fares need to be set well above bus fares if costs are to be recovered and heavy subsidies avoided.

4 PARATRANSIT AND TAXIS

PARATRANSIT

"Paratransit" - the term applied to small passenger transport vehicles operating informally on a fare-paying basis - proliferates throughout the Third World (see Plate 4.1 and Table 4.1). Often it is a valuable supplement, and in some places an alternative, to regular bus transit services. The emergence and rapid expansion of paratransit has arisen in many cities because of the decline in effectiveness and viability of public sector services. As discussed in Chapter 2, public sector services have relied heavily on subsidies which generally have not been able to keep up with growing demand. The resulting large gap in supply has been readily filled by private operators.

Paratransit systems are characterized by the variety of popular services they offer. They take several forms, from personalized door-to-door service and shared services with routes determined by individual passengers, to regular services along fairly well-defined routes. Paratransit also comprises a great variety of vehicles, such as pedal or motor rickshaws (Delhi); converted vans and pickups ("matatus" in Nairobi); converted jeeps ("jeepneys" in Manila); shared taxis ("dolmus" in Istanbul) and minibuses ("publicos" in Puerto Rico). They carry from 4 to 20 passengers in crush conditions. Journey speeds of motorized paratransit vehicles range from 12 - 20 kmph. The costs of the higher capacity paratransit run at about US 2 cents to 4 cents per passenger-km: about the same as small buses. Costs of smaller paratransit vehicles may run as

TABLE 4.1
Paratransit in selected cities: fleet size and share of the market

City	Type	Fleet Size	Share of motorised trips (%)
Delhi	Auto-rickshaws: converted scooters	28000	20
	Pedal rickshaws	5000	-
Istanbul	"Dolmus": shared 5 and 7 seat taxis.	16000	}
	Minibuses	4000	} 50
Jos	Shared Taxis	1900	}
	"Donfo" minibuses	250	} 60
Manila	"Jeepnies": shared taxis (based on military Jeeps)	28000	54
Nairobi	"Matatus": mainly converted pickups	2000	50
Surabaya	"Bemos": 10 seater minibuses	3200	30
	"Becaks": tricycle pedicabs	38000	-

Source: Jane's Urban Transport Systems 1991 and author's field notes

25

Plate 4.1a   Becaks (cycle rickshaws) in Surabaya, Indonesia

Plate 4.1b   Auto-rickshaws: New Delhi, India

Plate 4.1c   The Manila 'Jeepney': an example of the main urban public transport type in the Philippines

Plate 4.1d   Minibuses are used in many cities: an example from Freetown, Sierra Leone

27

Plate 4.1e   The 'tempo' of India

high as US 10 cents per passenger-km. In places where extreme over-loading occurs, as is the case of matatus in Nairobi, costs may be as low as US one cent per passenger-km (Box 4.1).

Generally, paratransit operators are free to choose vehicles, routes, frequency and hours of operation. But fares may be regulated, and in some cities congested routes are barred to paratransit.

Paratransit operators are responsive to the needs of the public and adapt quickly to changing patterns of demand. Because of their small size, paratransit vehicles are able to provide frequent and viable service at low levels of demand. Often, small paratransit vehicles are the only form of transport able to penetrate the labyrinth of narrow streets sometimes found in the old parts of cities and in squatter areas. Paratransit is particularly advantageous in areas where demand is insufficient to support the use of large buses at desirable frequencies.

Almost without exception, paratransit is operated by individual private owners or small enterprises, is highly competitive, and is run at a profit. As a result, paratransit places very little burden on city finances. In some places, with the growth in demand and increased financial returns, the tendency has been to discard make-shift vehicles and to move towards the use of imported minibuses, in many cases, with bodies built locally. In many cities, paratransit vehicles are perceived as being highly dangerous. This is because of poor driving and maintenance standards, and overloading. While paratransit accident rates may be a cause of concern, their dangerous reputation arises more from their proliferation and haste, rather than from sound statistical evidence. For example, in Karachi restrictions have been imposed on the number of minibuses on safety grounds. Because of the very large number of minibuses, they have a high

NAIROBI PARATRANSIT   BOX 4.1

Nairobi, the capital of Kenya, has a population of close to 2 million and an annual growth rate well in excess of 5 per cent. The rapid expansion of the population and spread of the urban area of Nairobi in recent years has put a very considerable strain on the public transport system and the road network. As a result bus services are overloaded and roads in the centre and along commuter corridors are heavily congested during peak periods. By far the majority of commuters are low income workers.

Motorized trips in Nairobi are roughly split equally between private cars (34 per cent), buses (36 per cent) and paratransit (30 per cent). At least 25 per cent of all trips are made on foot - some of them being in excess of 10 kilometres.

Public transport in Nairobi is provided by the private sector comprising large buses operated by a franchised bus company, Kenya Bus Services (KBS) and a large paratransit fleet of small buses and converted pickups, called matatus. There is also a public sector bus system operated by the National Youth Services (NYS). Although KBS runs efficient services, it has faced financial difficulties in recent years because of the need to keep fares low, and far from needed expansion, its fleet has diminished and now stands at about 250 buses. NYS is expanding with capital support from the Government. Its current fleet of 150 large buses in Nairobi has little impact on demand and is operating at a very considerable loss. By contrast, paratransit services have greatly expanded in recent years to about 2000 matatus and seem to thrive in the difficult traffic and financial conditions faced by public transport in Nairobi.

Matatus operate informal para-transit services with an element of route control exercised by operators associations. Access to the market is free and they are allowed to compete with KBS and NYS. They carry about 260,000 passengers daily and generally work the feeder routes and secondary roads, while KBS and NYS concentrate on the main corridors.

Originally matatus were mainly converted pickups, but in recent years these mostly have been replaced by 12 and 25 seat minibuses usually with locally made bodies. Almost without exception matatus are severely over-loaded, roughly handled and poorly maintained. As a result they last only two or three years before having to be replaced or rebuilt. There is also serious concern for the safety of passengers although there is a lack of concrete evidence to show that matatus suffer a higher accident rate than other vehicles in Kenya. Generally, matatu owners own only one or two vehicles, but a few own small fleets. Due to a lack of financial standing, owners find it difficult to purchase additional or replacement vehicles. So although there has been a big expansion in the number of matatus, this has been inhibited by a lack of finance and does not reflect the level of demand.

Because of low operating costs and very high load factors, fares on matatus are low at about US 10 cents for a 5 kilometre trip. Although the quality of service may leave much to be desired, matatus go a long way towards meeting the transport demands of the large low income groups at affordable fares.

profile, and together with hostility to drivers on ethnic grounds, have been saddled with a reputation of being dangerous. Government records actually show that minibuses in Karachi are involved in less accidents than the much smaller fleet of standard buses.

Paratransit operators often face considerable hostility from transport authorities because of their haphazard and undisciplined mode of operation which can cause considerable congestion. However, paratransit is generally very popular with users and very cost effective, and is likely to continue to be well established despite official opposition.

TAXIS

Taxis, operating in a variety of ways, are found in very large numbers throughout the developing world. Probably the most common are shared taxis, in which several passengers, not in the same party, are carried together and pay separate fares. Nevertheless, sizable fleets of conventional taxis, (for the exclusive use of the hirer) are found in many cities. Taxis may switch between being exclusive and shared depending on demand and the judgement of operators. In some places this is permitted, in others it is illegal, but widely practised. While taxis are often fitted with meters by regulation, the actual use of these meters to determine fares is quite rare. Instead fares are negotiated for each trip or based on a going rate. The fate of taxi meters is well illustrated by the situation with the taxis in Bangkok which number some 15000. Here, the use of meters lapsed some time ago because the regulated fare schedules did not keep pace with inflation and were too high for short trips and too low for long trips. So one way or another, the scheduled fares were unacceptable to either users or operators. Now fares are negotiated, with the going rate greatly exceeding bus and minibus fares. Operators are prepared to cruise for a high paying client rather than undercut the going rate. Accra provides an example of a typical taxi system (Box 4.2).

One of the largest fleets of taxis is found in Santiago, Chile, with over 40000 shared and conventional taxis. Taxi fares are 5 or 6 times bus fares and more than 10 times the subsidized metro fares. Nevertheless, taxis are able to capture about 0.5 million passengers per day - more than the metro and 6 per cent of the market. In a number of secondary cities, for example, Jos in Nigeria, taxis are virtually the only means of passenger transport available. Generally the modal share of motorised trips by taxis is in the region of 3 to 10 per cent but, may be as high as 20 per cent, as for example in Harare, Zimbabwe.

The very large number of taxis in some cities is often an indication, on the one hand, that bus services are inadequate, and on the other hand, that many passengers are prepared to pay more for more convenient or reliable transport and would pay more for better bus services.

ACCRA, GHANA: TAXIS   BOX 4.2

Fairly typical of taxi operations in the Third World are those in Accra, Ghana where the total fleet amounts to some 5000 taxis. These comprise small taxis carrying 3-5 passengers and larger cars that can take up to 8 passengers. All of these are un-metered and operate either on a shared ride basis along fixed routes or as exclusive taxis at premium fares. Shared taxis are particularly active in areas and along routes poorly served by buses and minibuses. In low density areas they are often the only means of motorized transport. Taxis are permitted unrestricted entry into the market, but in practice, operators obtain the agreement of their union before operating specific routes. The unions provide various services for their members including the management of taxi terminals. Taxi operators who are non-union members are deterred from using terminals and from operating certain routes. Taxi operators in Accra are required to obtain a taxi license for their vehicles and taxis are subject to 6 monthly vehicle inspections. However, from the very poor condition of taxis, it is evident that inspections are superficial and not vigorously enforced. Taxi fares are regulated by the Government and are based on distance. Shared taxi fares for each passenger are 2.5 times bus fares but are close to 10 times the bus fare for exclusive use.

5 BUSWAY TRANSIT

In order to improve performance of bus services, and to cope with heavy demand along major commuter corridors, a number of Third World cities (mainly in Brazil but also in Peru, Turkey and Cote d'Ivoire) have introduced busways. These are segregated traffic lanes for the exclusive use of buses. Busway transit comprises a system of busways, generally using high capacity buses, with some form of management or control organisation. Various means of collecting and distributing passengers beyond the busway facility may be employed. With special operational measures, busway transit can provide a highly efficient and cost effective system of mass transit (Table 5.1 (a) and (b)).

Busways have mainly been introduced along existing roads but in a few places have been purpose-built. In either case, they generally consist of two lanes (one in each direction) and sometimes incorporate additional lanes at bus stops to permit overtaking. Unlike bus-only lanes, busways provide buses with physical separation from other traffic by use of barriers such as medians, high kerbs or studs. In some cases, fences also are provided along busways to keep out pedestrians. Busways may be located in the middle of the carriageway (for example Sao Paulo) or next to the kerbs (Istanbul). Where busways intersect with other roads, buses may be given priority over other traffic by the use of specially phased or controlled traffic signals. However, this has not proved to be feasible where priority for an almost continuous flow of buses (about one every 12 seconds in Porto Alegre) would completely disrupt crossing traffic. Elevated or grade separated busways would provide a solution but have yet to be constructed in any Third World city. However, elevated and grade separated busways are planned for Bangkok, Karachi and elsewhere.

THE PERFORMANCE OF BUSWAY TRANSIT

The performance of busway transit varies considerably from place to place and depends on a large number of factors. Of particular influence are the extent to which overtaking is permitted, the bus stop arrangements, the capacity of the buses, special operational measures such as the ordering of buses, and the proportion of boarding to alighting passengers.

Without any special operational measures and using standard buses, busways are found to carry about 10,000 passengers per hour in one direction (p/h/d) in standard buses and 15,000 p/h/d in high capacity buses. Flows of over 19,500 p/h/d have been recorded on the basic busway in Abidjan, but with extensive bus queuing and crush loading. Where special operational measures exist, in particular where there is provision for buses to overtake at stops, flows are generally in the range of 15,000 - 18,000 or more. However much higher flows have been recorded under favourable conditions. For example, flows of more that 20,000 p/h/d occur in Sao Paulo, while in Porto Alegre, passenger flows regularly exceed 26,000 p/h/d (Plate 5.1).

TABLE 5.1
Examples of Third World busways

(a) Characteristics of selected busways

City	Busway scheme	Length surveyed (km)	Average stop spacing (m)	Average junction spacing (m)	Special features
Abidjan	Blvd de la Republique	1.3	400	160	none
Ankara	Besevler-Dikinevi	3.6	310	410	none
Belo Horizonte	Av Cristiano Machado	8.6	610	920	overtaking at stops
Curitiba	Eixo Sul	9.5	370	430	trunk & feeder
Istanbul	Taksim-Zincirlikuyu	2.8	310	410	none
Porto Alegre	Assis Brasil	4.5	560	430	bus ordering
Porto Alegre	Farrapapos	2.8	560	390	bus ordering
Sao Paulo	Av 9 de Julho	7.9	600	530	overtaking at stops

(b) Summary of the performance of selected busways

City	Busway	Peak bus flows (bus/hour in one direction)		Peak available passenger places (pass/hour in one direction)		Peak passenger flows (pass/hour in one direction)		Average commercial bus speed (kmph)	
		am	pm	am	pm	am	pm	am	pm
Abidjan	Bvld de la Republique	204	197	20200	19500	16000	19500	12.8	8.0
Ankara	Besevler-Dikiaevi	91	91	7300	7300	7300	6500	12.0	10.4
Belo Horizonte	Av Cris. Machado	216	215	19200	18200	15800	14500	24.6	29.3
Curitaba	Eixo Sul	94	80	11400	9800	9900	7000	21.0	21.3
Istanbul	Taksim-Zincirlikuyu	169	143	12800	11000	10700	7300	14.0	11.3
Porto Alegre	Assis Brasil	326	260	33600	27000	26100	18300	22.7	17.8
Porto Alegre	Farrapos	378	304	39400	32300	15300	17500	21.9	19.7
Sao Paulo	Av 9 de Julho	230	221	20300	19400	18600	20300	19.6	16.3

Source: TRL Research Report 329

Because of the intensity of use of busways in Third World cities, there are very high passenger movements at bus stops. Boardings or alightings at busway bus stops of between 1000 to 2000 passengers per hour are not uncommon, and are well above those generally found in Europe and North America. At a number of places even higher volumes occur; for example, at the Kizilay bus stop in Ankara during the evening peak there are in the region of 3000 passengers per hour boarding and a similar number alighting (Table 5.2).

For well designed busways, bus flows are often more than 200 per hour in one direction (h/d): they are as high as 378 h/d during the morning peak hour on the well ordered Farapos busway in Porto Alegre. Elsewhere in Brazil and in Abidjan bus flows of about 200 h/d are regularly achieved in both the AM and PM peaks. In the case of Ankara, bus flows are much lower at less that 100 h/d. This is due not only to the low allocation of buses but also due to the lack of provision

Plate 5.1a   A busway in Porto Alegre, Brazil

Plate 5.1b   Buses queuing on the busway at Kizilay Square bus stand, Ankara, Turkey

TABLE 5.2
Busway bus stops: comparative passenger movements

City	Location	am/pm Peak	Passengers/hour		Buses/ hour
			boarding	alighting	
Ankara	Kizilay: westbound	pm	3345	1020	61
	eastbound	pm	2880	3136	72
Istanbul	Osmanbey	am	380	4020	139
Abidjan	Jardin St Paul	am	785	3036	202
Sao Paulo	Estados Unidos	am	260	1580	195
Porto Alegre	Centro Commercial	am	340	1515	304
Curitiba	Portao	pm	390	1205	91
Belo Horizonte	Primenta de Veiga	am	605	25	108

Source: TRL Research Report 329

for overtaking, and to congestion at junctions and stops. The average journey speeds of buses on busways in city centres where bus stops and intersections are closely spaced, are in the region of 8 - 14 kmph. Elsewhere on busways average journey speeds are as high as 17 - 30 kmph (Figure 5.1).

BUSWAY OPERATIONS

Most busway operations are subject to only conventional traffic management and enforcement. However, on a number of busways, special controls are employed. For example, in Sao Paulo and Porto Alegre, buses are dispatched in a set order (termed bus ordering), and stop opposite a series of designated bus stops in a predetermined sequence (Plate 5.2). This avoids passengers having to scramble from one part of the stopping area to another as buses arrive. Several buses can thus proceed with boarding and alighting at the same time. As a result, delays to buses at bus stops are greatly reduced and passenger flows and journey speeds are increased. A more sophisticated variation of bus ordering, (termed COMONOR), involves buses operating in convoys, moving off and stopping in unison like rail cars in a train. COMONOR was introduced into Sao Paulo (Box 5.1) and Porto Alegre but was found to be too difficult to be sustained. Bus ordering and convoy systems are dependent on a high level of driver and passenger discipline which may be difficult to achieve under the conditions experienced in many Third World cities.

In some cities, for example Curitiba, Brazil, trunk-and-feeder systems operate in which passengers from the surrounding area are carried by feeder buses to a busway terminal or station, where they transfer to the large trunk buses using the busway. The process is reversed on the return journey. Transfers between feeder and trunk buses are made in a closed area with no further payment of fares. This reduces cost, and to some extent overcomes the inconvenience to passengers of having to transfer. Since no ticket validation is necessary and all four doors of the articulated trunk buses can be used, boarding can be very quick. However heavy reliance is placed on the close cooperation of the bus companies operating this type of system, and on the support

34

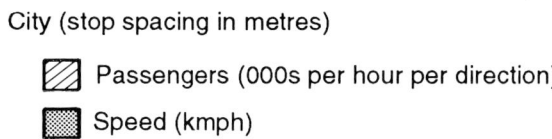

City (stop spacing in metres)

Passengers (000s per hour per direction)

Speed (kmph)

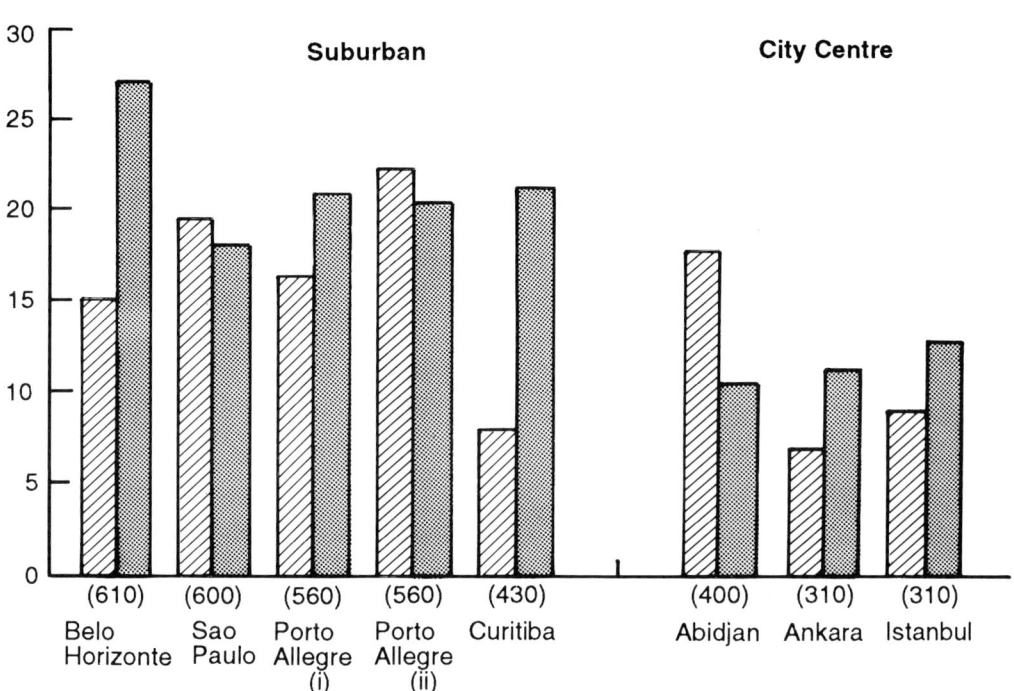

Source: TRL Research Report 329

Fig 5.1   Busway commercial speeds and passenger flows

of the public. In the case of Porto Alegre, the trunk-and-feeder operations had to be abandoned. This was due to a conflict with bus operators' concessions and passenger resistance to enforced interchanging. It is for these or similar reasons that on most busway transit systems, the routes of buses using the busways extend well beyond the busway. In this way passengers are collected and dispersed throughout the city with the minimum of interchanging. Since under these arrangements buses can join and leave busways at intermediate points as well as at the ends, a very wide passenger catchment area is served by busway transit.

Busway transit provides considerable flexibility, particularly compared to rail systems. It can be more readily adjusted and enhanced step by step to meet the inevitable changes in demand for quantity and quality which characterise Third World development. This flexibility is evident from the wide range of demands met by busway transit (from 7000 to 26000 p/h/d), the choice of services provided, and the wide variety of buses operated. Most busway transit systems include

35

Plate 5.2   Buses travelling along a busway in an ordered group

express, coach and local bus services. The buses operated include high capacity buses such as double deckers, articulated buses and trolley buses, and large and medium size single deck buses. Generally, minibuses and paratransit vehicles are excluded from busways.

While the infrastructure is generally provided by central or city governments, busways are used mainly by private sector bus operators. In a number of places busways are shared with the public bus corporation. For example, in Sao Paulo the state bus company, CMTC and several private companies all use the busway. CMTC also manages and regulates the busway. In Abidjan buses using the busway are operated by a single company, SOTRA, jointly owned by the State and a multi-national vehicle manufacturer.

COSTS

The infrastructure for at-grade busways along existing rights-of-way, including terminals, costs in the region of US$1 million to US$2 million per kilometre. Rolling stock costs depend on the type of vehicle and are similar to the rolling stock costs for conventional bus services. Because of more efficient operation, the costs per passenger using busway transit are little more than for conventional bus services: in some cases costs are less. Efficient systems represent very considerable economic saving and since busways can be constructed and maintained with locally available labour and materials, and using locally assembled buses, the foreign exchange requirement is minimised.

The capital costs of busways compare very favourably with those of rail systems which may be between 5 and 50 times the costs of busways, and in some cases even more. (The costs of rail systems are reviewed in the chapters which follow). As a result of their high capacity and cost effectiveness, busways provide a very attractive transit option for Third World cities, particularly in the face of the increasing scarcity of resources. Also the success of the Brazilian busways has stimulated considerable interest in industrialized as well as in developing countries.

6 RAIL MASS TRANSIT: METROS

Many Third World cities have some form of rail mass transit. While there are considerable differences between systems, they generally fall within the following main types (as defined in World Bank Technical Paper No. 52):-

Metros (The more common term for rail rapid transit, and sometimes called subways or "the underground"). Metros operate on completely segregated rights-of-way at high speeds and high capacity. Passengers board from high level platforms to facilitate rapid loading. Vehicles operate in trains of four to ten cars. (eg Calcutta Metro: Box 6.1; Mexico City metro: Box 6.2)

Light Rail Transit. These systems range from trams operating in mixed traffic along public streets to semi-metros on exclusive tracks. Passengers usually board from the road or from low platforms, and vehicles operate in single units or in short trains at slow to moderate speeds. (eg Tunis LRT: Box 7.3)

Suburban Rail Transit. (Sometimes called commuter railways). These usually operate on tracks shared with inter-city trains and freight trains. Rolling stock may be similar to heavy inter-city trains or may be of the metro type. (eg. Bombay: Box 8.1)

This chapter reviews the state of the art in respect of metros: separate chapters on LRT and suburban rail follow. The maximum passenger flows of these systems, compared with busways, are illustrated in Figure 6.1.

With a strong desire to overcome severe traffic congestion and deteriorating bus services, and spurred on by manufacturers, Third World city authorities have increasingly turned to rail mass transit, with particular emphasis on metros. However, for many years metros were comparatively rare in the Third World. Exceptions are the long established metros in Buenos Aires (1913), Beijing (1969) and Mexico City (1969). But an upsurge of interest in metros over the last 15 years has seen a dramatic increase. At the present time there are almost 20 metros in operation in Third World cities and a similar number are at the planning and design stage. Some six new systems are under construction and several existing systems are being extended.

Despite this growing interest, the success of metros has been very mixed. A recent detailed study by TRL has shown that there is a marked divergence between the expected benefits of metros and the actual achievements. While metros have generally reduced overcrowding, lowered waiting times and provided faster journeys, in most cases expected reductions in road congestion and in the use of private cars have not materialized or at best have been short lived. In addition, financial performance has mostly fallen well short of targets, leading to very heavy capital and operational subsidies. With benefits closely linked to income levels, only in the higher income cities were economic returns found to be at acceptable levels. Major benefits have been confined mainly to higher income passengers who can afford to use the metro.

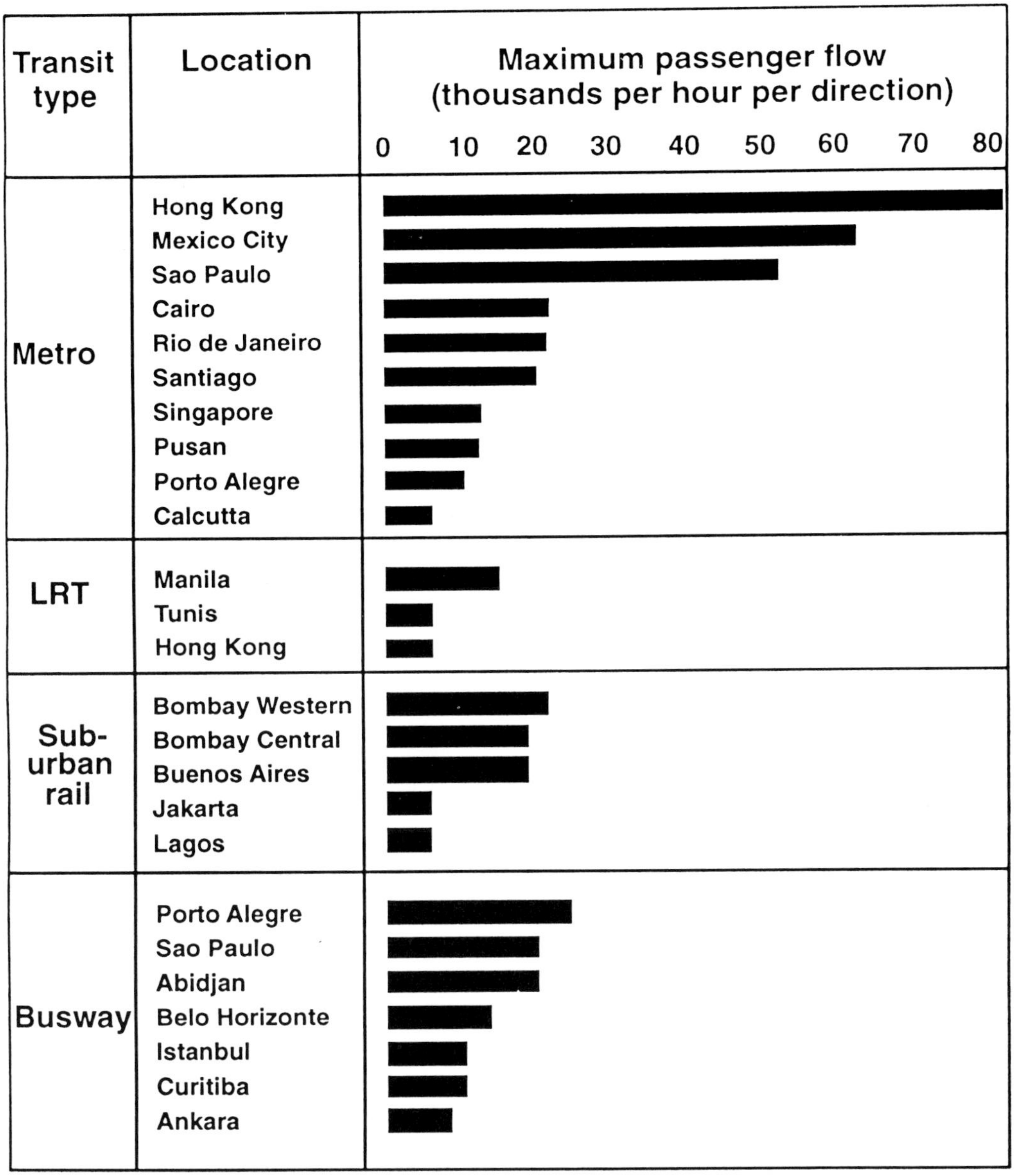

Transit type	Location	Maximum passenger flow (thousands per hour per direction)
		0 10 20 30 40 50 60 70 80
Metro	Hong Kong	████████████████████████████████
	Mexico City	████████████████████████
	Sao Paulo	█████████████████████
	Cairo	█████████
	Rio de Janeiro	█████████
	Santiago	█████████
	Singapore	██████
	Pusan	██████
	Porto Alegre	█████
	Calcutta	██
LRT	Manila	██████
	Tunis	██
	Hong Kong	██
Sub-urban rail	Bombay Western	████████
	Bombay Central	███████
	Buenos Aires	███████
	Jakarta	██
	Lagos	██
Busway	Porto Alegre	█████████
	Sao Paulo	████████
	Abidjan	████████
	Belo Horizonte	█████
	Istanbul	████
	Curitiba	████
	Ankara	███

Source: TRL Research Report 329 and author's research

Fig 6.1   Mass Transit Maximum Passenger Flows

METRO CHARACTERISTICS

Most of the metros in Third World cities are in the European tradition using high speed and capacity technology and generally operating underground. Many are limited to one or two, usually short, radial lines. Exceptions are the networks in Buenos Aires (40km), Mexico City (141km), Seoul (116km) and Hong Kong (43km) (Plate 6.1).

Plate 6.1   The Hong Kong Mass Transit Railway

Journey speeds for metros generally range between 30 and 35 kmph. with the stations spaced 1.0 to 1.3km apart. Higher journey speeds are usually associated with more widely spaced stations as in the case of Porto Alegre with journey speeds of 42kmph and an average station spacing of 1.9 km. The systems vary in capacity from 27,000 to 75,000 p/h/d. At the higher capacities, train headways are 2 minutes or slightly less (Table 6.1).

The positioning of metros has a strong influence on the numbers of people travelling on the system. In Hong Kong, the location of the metro within walking distance of some of the densest urban development in the world has resulted in highly intensive use. On the other hand, while the metro in Porto Alegre provides an excellent low-fare service and is supported by a network of feeder buses, it has a mediocre catchment area with a relatively small population within walking distance. Much of the anticipated development which the Porto Alegre metro was to serve has not materialised. Most critically of all, the route, which follows an old railway line, terminates too far from the city centre to meet effectively the travel needs of central area commuters.

TABLE 6.1
Characteristics of selected full metros

City	capital cost US$m /km	percent under-ground %	Length km	Station spacing km	Minimum headway min:sec	Cars per train	Hourly design capacity p/h/d	Average journey speed kmph
Cairo	13	11	42.5	1.3	2:30	6/9	60,000	-
Calcutta	26	95	16.5	1.0	2:10	8	59,000	33
Hong Kong:								
Kowloon	64	77	26.0	1.1	2:00	8	75,000	33
Island	106	84	12.5	1.0	3:30	7	38,000	33
Mexico City	30	75	131.0	1.2	1:55	9	46,000	35
Porto Alegre	10	0	26.7	1.9	6:00	4/8/12	16,000	41
Pusan	32	79	32.0	1.0	2:00	6	27,000	32
Rio de Janeiro	83	100	11.6	0.8	3:00	6	45,000	29
Santiago	36	81	26.0	0.7	2:40	5	20,000	32
Sao Paulo:								
Line 1	80	82	17.0	0.9	1:45	6	58,000	29
Line 2	-	32	11.5	1.2	1:50	6	48,000	38
Seoul	45	80	116.5	1.2	3:00	6	29,000	36.5
Singapore	37	30	67.0	1.6	2:00	6	-	-

Source:TRL Research Report 278 and author's research.

Fares structures and integration of bus and metro fares similarly have a strong influence on patronage. Fare integration, (ie one fare payment for a journey combining trips on both bus and metro), is designed to reduce the cost to passengers where flat fares apply, and to reduce the inconvenience of interchanging between modes. As a result it can greatly increase patronage particularly from suburban and industrial areas not within walking distance of the metro. Most third world cities with metros have developed plans to improve patronage through integration. However, generally these have not been implemented or if implemented have not proved to be effective. Sao Paulo is the only city in which a successful system of integration seems to have been achieved, with bus and metro serving the same corridor and about 50 per cent of all metro passengers transferring to or from buses. However, this has been achieved only at the cost of a substantial operating subsidy for the metro.

Measures to protect metros from bus competition, often based on dubious justifications, similarly have not worked in practice. The exceptions are Mexico City, where metro fares were, until recently, set at artificially low levels bearing little relation to the actual cost of a journey, and Tunis, where the LRT has virtually replaced the buses by offering a better service at the same fare. Elsewhere the task of removing bus competition has proved intractable in the face of an unwilling public and uncooperative bus operators. In Cairo, for example, the metro and the buses are administered by two separate government organisations: because the metro fares are so much higher than the bus fares, there is no real possibility of eliminating buses. A similar situation of grossly unequal fares applies in Calcutta. When the Hong Kong mass rapid transit railway (MTR) opened to disappointingly low levels of patronage, the government attempted to redeploy buses and minibuses but was largely unsuccessful; now MTR patronage is so high that there is less case for trying to remove the bus competition.

41

Only a few city authorities have attempted to build up metro patronage by planning for high-density housing development in the metro corridor or encouraging the growth of employment centres to be served by the metro. The clearest examples are in Hong Kong and Singapore, where the importance of integrated land use and transport planning has long been recognised as a means of obtaining a more efficient structure of development and a better match between social needs and transport supply. In some cities there were expectations that new urban development would follow the arrival of the metro, but these were often based on broad-brush strategies for distant planning horizons, and have yet to materialise. Experience in developed countries indicates that the development benefits of metros are closely linked to the existence of well established central plans and strong city-wide transport authorities. These are often lacking in developing cities. While metros have been found to enhance development where conditions are already favourable for private investment, they do little to a assist areas suffering from economic decline.

OWNERSHIP AND MANAGEMENT

In most Third World cities, while ownership is in the hands of government at either national, regional or metropolitan level, a new organisation - usually a public corporation - has been established to manage and operate the metro. Generally the intention is that these organisations should be independent of government services, in particular, of national railways. These are inclined to follow inflexible and outmoded practices and are not geared to the dynamic style of operations so vital for metro viability. But the independence of most metro operating agencies is severely limited by the fact that none of the metros is financially fully self-supporting.

CONSTRUCTION

In view of their massive size, metro schemes generally have attracted international consultants for project design and management, and international contractors for construction. Invariably the supply of rolling stock and other equipment has been subject to intense international competition. This has generally resulted in sound engineering and high quality rolling stock. However, apart from Singapore, Seoul and Hong Kong, most systems have been subject to excessive time over-runs. Average construction periods are in the region of 8 years compared to planned completion within 5 years. In the case of Calcutta, progress has been less than one kilometre per year (11 years for the first 10 km phase, 17 years for the 16.4 km system as a whole) (see Plate 6.2 and Box 6.1).

The metro systems in Third World cities are mainly operated on either 750V dc or 1.5kV dc electrical supply and are almost equally divided between overhead and third rail systems. The rubber tyred systems of Mexico City and Santiago rely on dual lateral guide rails for power collection. The Hong Kong system was originally designed with third rail power collection to minimise the size and cost of tunnels. This was changed to an overhead system because of the risks in the depots and to speed the evacuation of passengers from trains stopped in tunnels because of emergencies. It was anticipated that anxiety over the possibility of the third rail being live or becoming live could impede evacuation. It has been estimated that because of seasonal high ambient temperatures and humidity in Hong Kong, heavily loaded trains would need to be

Plate 6.2   The Metro Railway, Calcutta

evacuated within 15 minutes of any stoppages in tunnels involving ventilation failure. This problem was alleviated in Singapore by use of a bottom contact third rail system but continues to be a source of serious concern in high temperature cities, such as Calcutta, using live third rails in their underground systems.

Because of their complete reliance on electricity for operation, control and ventilation, metro services are seriously disrupted by power cuts.

In order to obtain the very high speeds and capacities required, (and with the encouragement of suppliers), the construction and operation of metros involve highly sophisticated technology. Rarely has this been matched by existing local experience and skills. As a result heavy reliance has been placed on the use of expatriate staff sometimes on a long term basis. Advanced cities, such as Hong Kong and Singapore have successfully undertaken extensive training programmes for operational and maintenance staff. Nevertheless, they have found it necessary to continue to employ a number of full time expatriates.

METRO ROLLING STOCK

Most Third World metros consist of six to eight-car trains. Notable exceptions are Mexico City and Cairo with nine car trains and Santiago with five-car trains. Generally metro trains are

The Calcutta Metro can claim to be amongst the very few metros that have relied almost entirely on national technology and expertise. Apart from employment of foreign consultants for advice on complex tunnelling problems, the system was largely built by Indian engineers, technicians and workers using mainly Indian materials and equipment. The system is clearly a source of pride and is treated with respect by the users: there is very little littering, spitting or vandalism and the high standard of cleanliness of the metro is in sharp contrast to other services and facilities in Calcutta. However, the system has been beset by many problems and inordinate construction delays. These arise more from planning, funding and policy making issues than from technical problems.

Construction of the 16.4 km metro commenced as early as 1973, however the first two separate sections of the metro, totalling 10 km, were not opened until 1984. The remaining 6.4 km section, which links the first two sections, is not expected to be completed much before 1995. The system is almost entirely underground.

The metro has a stock of 144 cars operating in 8-car trains designed to carry approximately 2500 passengers each. Power supply is 750 V dc fed by third rail. Because of the high temperatures experienced in Calcutta, the stations and tunnels are ventilated by forced cooled air. The control of trains is exercised through a central control room with cab signalling and automatic train protection.

While 2.5 minute headway are planned (later to be reduced to 1.5 minutes) currently headway are 12 minutes during the peak and as long as 20 minutes off-peak. Also, operation is for only 13.5 hours each day which is considerably less than for other metros. Clearly, until the linking section is completed, the full potential of the system, planned at 1.7 million passengers per day, cannot be achieved. In the meantime total patronage is only 65,000 daily, which is well below the capacity of the two completed sections. One of the reasons for low patronage is the fact that fares on the metro, at US 8 cents for up to 5km and US 12 cents for over 5km, are double the fares on buses and trams. This is a major consideration in a city where the great majority of commuters are on very low incomes, and have to put cost saving before convenience, comfort and safety.

Capital costs of the metro are several times the original estimates and on completion of the whole 16.4 km are expected to be in the region of US$700 million. Income in 1987 was US$ 1.5 million and total operating costs (including depreciation) were estimated to be at least US$ 5.4 million. A simplified economic evaluation of the completed system indicates a very low economic rate of return of 2.8 per cent. This poor return is explained by a combination of adverse factors - low levels of patronage, low value of time and high capital costs, inflated in economic terms as a result of long construction delays.

comprised of electric multiple units (EMUs) operating in pairs or three car sets. Car layouts are usually designed to maximize loading with emphasis on standing areas and limited seating.

SIGNALLING AND CONTROL

Metro systems designed to achieve high speeds and frequency of operation with reliability and safety, involve some form of sophisticated signalling and control systems. For example, Sao Paulo (Plate 6.3) with 110 second headway and aiming for 90 second headway, uses automatic train supervision (ATS) and automatic train operation (ATO), with a centralised control centre. Caracas, with 90 second headway is controlled by full automatic train control (ATC).

Plate 6.3   The Metro of Sao Paulo, Brazil

METRO OPERATIONAL PERFORMANCE

The established networks show a wide variation both in annual ridership from 139m passengers in Santiago to 1450m in Mexico City, and in peak hourly flows from 20,000 p/h/d in Santiago to 81,000 p/h/d in Hong Kong. The ridership statistics are dominated by the performance of the Mexico City metro, with average daily boardings of more than 4.5m (Box 6.2).

A number of metros in the Third World are used very intensively. The Sao Paulo metro and Hong Kong MTR produce annual utilisation rates of over 17 million and 13.8 million passengers per route km respectively, making the Sao Paulo system the most intensively used metro system in the world. By way of comparison, the world's two most extensive systems in terms of route length - London and New York - have rates of only 1.4m and 2.9m passengers/km respectively (Table 6.2).

On most metro systems the aim is to maintain headways no greater than about 2 minutes in the peaks. In Sao Paulo, where at key stations passengers simultaneously alight and board from platforms either side of the car, headways of 1.75 minutes are consistently achieved over the peak period. Apart from Sao Paulo, intervals of 2 minutes or less occur only in Hong Kong and Mexico City. At these headways all three metro systems are operating at the limits of their practical capacity. Elsewhere peak headways range from 2.5 minutes to 12 minutes. Overcrowding in the peaks is common on most metros, and in some, notably Mexico City and Hong Kong, it is a cause for concern.

While often well utilized, even the largest metros in Third World cities, as in industrialized cities,

MEXICO CITY METRO   BOX 6.2

The population of Mexico City, in the region of 20 million, is by far the largest of any metropolitan area in the Third World and is rapidly overtaking the Tokyo-Yokohama complex as the most populated conurbation worldwide. As such, it generates enormous demand for passenger transport of all types. The Mexico City Metro, with the most extensive network in the Third World, makes a very important contribution towards meeting this demand. Nevertheless, while the patronage at over 4.5 million trips per day is amongst the highest of all metros, just as many trips are made by car and more than twice as many again are made by bus.

Since its opening in 1969, the metro has been progressively extended and improved, and now comprises a network of 8 lines, 125 stations and has a route length of 140 km. Most of this length is underground (91km). A comparatively small part is elevated (15km) and the remainder is at grade.

The system, which is based on French technology, uses rolling stock mainly manufactured locally in Mexico but also imported from France and Canada. Rolling stock comprises 2300 rubber-tyred cars formed into nine-car trains powered by 750 volts via dual lateral guide bars. In order to achieve very close headways, which are less than 2 minutes during peak periods, the system incorporates electronic automatic train operation and line control systems.

Several radial lines, (numbers 1,2 and 3), are often heavily overloaded with each regularly carrying up to 65,000 passengers per hour in one direction. Line 1, which carries 24 million passengers per kilometre each year, is probably the most intensively utilized metro line anywhere in the world. The remaining lines are transversal and generally are poorly utilized and difficult to justify.

The funding of the Mexico City Metro has come mainly from France in the form of soft loans from the French Government and commercial loans from French Banks. Capital costs of Lines 1, 2 and 3, totalling 66 km of route, have been estimated at close to US$ 2000 million (1986). Despite the fact that efficient operation has kept operating costs low and utilization very high, revenue is quite unable to cover even basic operating costs, let alone depreciation and interest. This is because fares have been held artificially low for social/political reasons, with no attempt, until recently, to relate fares to costs.

While the system as a whole may show poor financial and economic returns, the heavily utilised lines considered in isolation achieve a reasonable level of viability. The economic internal rate of return for Lines 1, 2, and 3 has been estimated at over 11 per cent.

Future plans include the extension of existing lines and the construction of additional lines which aim to increase the network to over 300 km by 2010.

generally carry only a modest proportion of the total public transport passengers. The Mexico City metro is estimated to serve 35 per cent of all passengers within the Distrito Federal, which includes less than half the population of the metropolitan area; in Santiago and Sao Paulo the proportion is 15 per cent. Furthermore, it is evident that metros have attracted only a very small proportion of motorists. Surveys in Porto Alegre (Plate 6.4) shortly after the metro opened indicated that only 4 per cent of the passengers had formerly travelled by car. With motor cars seen as a major status symbol, those who can afford them are reluctant to forego their use to travel in some discomfort with the urban masses.

TABLE 6.2
Indicators of metro system operational performance (1987)

System	Annual passengers carried		Peak Directional Load 000's/hour[5]	Average Trip Length km	Peak Headway min/sec
	Total (millions)	Per route km (millions)			
Cairo	150[3]	5.3	22	9 app	7'30"[4]
Calcutta	19	1.9	5 approx	6 app	12'
Hong Kong	532	13.8	81	9.3	2'
Mexico City	1450[2]	11.0	65	9 app	1'55"
Porto Alegre	36	1.3	11 approx	11.1	6'
Pusan	79	3.7	13	7.6	5'
Rio de Janeiro[1]	108	5.3	22	5.0	5'
- Line 1 only	102	9.1			
Santiago	139	5.3	20	5.4	2'40"
Sao Paulo	465	17.2	57	7.2	1'45"
Seoul	854	7.3	?	8.9	3'
Singapore[3]	80[2]	3.2	14	?	?

[1] 1988 data
[2] estimated from daily figures
[3] estimates for 1988

[4] early reduction to 6' planned
[5] at the busiest section of the route

Source: TRL Research Report 278

Plate 6.4   Depot and administration buildings of the Porto Alegre metro

47

COSTS

Nearly all the metro systems have incurred higher costs than expected, in real terms. Of the metros included in the TRL study, only the Hong Kong mass transit railway and Porto Alegre metro have so far been completed within budget, though they will probably be joined by the Singapore mass rapid transit system (when the recommended scheme is completed). Elsewhere, the picture is one of substantial cost over-runs. The total capital cost per kilometre of route ranges between US$22m and US$60m for elevated metros, while the total capital costs per km of underground metros are in the range US$50m-165m (all at 1987 prices). Thus comparatively small systems of 25km, typically part underground and part elevated, cost in the region of US$2000 million to US$3000 million.

In no Third World city is the full cost of building and running a metro recovered from the users. (Even in industrialized countries, the full costs are often not paid by the users). As a result the capital cost and operating costs of metros are heavily subsidized, usually by central governments. For example, annual operating losses, including depreciation but excluding initial capital costs amount to US$150m for Mexico City metro, US$80m for Sao Paulo and US$10m for Pusan. In Hong Kong, Singapore and Seoul, where users can afford much higher fares, income more than covers operating costs and is able to make a substantial contribution to financial charges. Nevertheless, each of these systems has required very large capital grants and other assistance from their central governments. In the case of Hong Kong, in addition to receiving government equity, the metro corporation was granted rights to develop the space above stations and depots. This yielded revenue amounting to over 10 per cent of railway construction costs, and provides rental income equivalent to about 5 per cent of fare box revenue.

The comparative financial performance of various metros is set out in Table 6.3. Since the figures do not include interest on borrowing, the total losses in most cases are much larger than indicated.

TABLE 6.3
Metro financial performance (US$ million per year)[1]

City	estimated metro income	estimated metro costs		estimated surplus		estimated per passenger		estimated farebox ratio
		operating	total[2]	over operating cost	over total cost	Income	Operating Cost	Revenue/ operating cost
						(US cents)		
Calcutta	1.5	3.4	5.4	-1.9	-3.9	8.1	18	0.4
Hong Kong	215.6	98.6	164.1	117.0	51.5	40.5	19	2.2
Mexico City	60.0	150.0	210.0	-90.0	-150.0	4.1	10	0.4
Porto Alegre	2.4	12.6	25.6	-10.2	-23.2	6.6	35	0.2
Pusan	15.5	15.77	25.7	-0.3	-10.2	20.7	20	1.0
Rio de Janeiro	12.5	25.0	35.0	-12.5	-22.5	11.3	23	0.5
Santiago	23.4	14.7	23.4	8.7	0.0	16.8	11	1.6
Sao Paulo	40.0	63.0	120.0	-23.0	-80.0	9.1	14	0.6
Seoul	183.7	128.7	157.8	55.0	25.9	21.5	15	1.4

[1] 1986 data for Hong Kong, Porto Alegre and Santiago
1987 for Calcutta, Pusan, Rio and Seoul
1988 estimates for Mexico City and Sao Paulo

[2] operating cost and depreciation
(excluding initial capital cost)
Source: TRL Research Report 278

ECONOMIC VIABILITY

An economic evaluation of 13 metros undertaken during the TRL study found three with economic rates of return less than 10 per cent, three between 10 and 12 per cent, four between 12 and 15 per cent, and three above 15 per cent. The results above 15 per cent, were for Singapore, Hong Kong and Cairo. Cairo is an exceptional case where the metro results from the linking and upgrading of two busy suburban lines. Thus with the single exception of Cairo, no metro in a developing city is expected to produce an economic return greater than 15 per cent.

The impressive rates of return calculated for Singapore (20 per cent) and Hong Kong (18 per cent) are influenced by the high incomes and values of time in those cities. The poor return calculated for the existing line in Calcutta (3 per cent) is explained by a combination of adverse factors - low levels of patronage, low value of time and high capital costs, inflated in economic terms as a result of long construction delays. The Rio de Janeiro system (7 per cent) showed a disappointing result again reflecting a history of protracted delays in funding and construction. The Santiago metro, of similar length, has a 14 per cent economic rate of return.

7 LIGHT RAIL TRANSIT

There are some twenty light rail transits (LRT) in Third World cities. More than half of these are long established conventional tramways, with capacities of little more than 6000 passengers per hour per direction. The remainder are of the more modern higher capacity systems - often termed LRT metros - designed for flows of up to 28,000 passengers per hour in each direction (Plate 7.1).

TRAMWAYS

At the height of their popularity, in the early part of the century, there were some 1500 tramways spread throughout the World. With the rapid growth of motor vehicles, in particular motor buses, little more than 300 tramways have survived the stiff competition for passengers and use of road space. In Third World cities, because rapid growth in demand mainly post-dates the heyday of the tramways, few tramways were ever established. Currently there are only about 15. Of these, the most notable are the large networks in Calcutta (71 km), Cairo (54 km) and Alexandria (31 km). Others generally range in length from 12 to 16 km and comprise two or three lines (Table 7.1).

Unlike metro and heavy rail trains, trams are able to negotiate comparatively sharp bends and steep inclines. This has permitted the installation of tramways in existing streets avoiding the need for costly civil works. Most tramways in Third World cities have followed this convention with trams generally operating in mixed traffic. In only a few places are trams provided with exclusive rights-of-way. In either case, passengers board from either low platforms at kerb level or directly from the road surface.

TABLE 7.1
Conventional tramways: major systems

City	Length (km)	Cars	Daily passenger trips
Anshan, China	12.9	77	270,000
Changchun, China	28.5	99	428,000
Dalian, China	14.8	104	600,000
Alexandria, Egypt	31.0	170	400,000
Cairo, Egypt	54.0	450	360,000
Hong Kong (Victoria)	16.3	162	335,000
Calcutta, India	71.0	428	630,000

Source: Tim V. Runnacles, Developing World Land Transport 1987, and author's research.

Plate 7.1a   Manila's elevated light rail transit system

Plate 7.1b   The new LRT in Tunis

Plate 7.1c   Two car tram set of Cairo Transport Authority

Plate 7.1d   Veteran trams still in use in Hong Kong

52

The rolling stock of tramways mainly comprises 4 axle cars or 6 axle articulated units, carrying between 100 and 200 passengers. Most operate in single units, are manually controlled and involve the minimum of signalling. In this configuration, in mixed traffic, tramways are able to carry 6000 passengers per hour per direction.

Power supply for tramways is via 500-750V dc overhead transmission systems. Like other electrically powered transit systems, tramways are vulnerable to power cuts. These are not infrequent in some developing countries, and when they occur, large sections of the tramway systems are brought to a standstill.

Under favourable traffic conditions, the location of low cost trams on-street, providing quick and easy access, has proved to be very popular with many passengers. For example, the on-street tramway in Hong Kong has continued to enjoy heavy and increasing patronage despite the opening of the underground mass transit Island Line over the same route. However most tramways in Third World cities face deteriorating conditions with services seriously disrupted by mounting traffic congestion. Even where rights-of-way are designated for the exclusive use of trams, other vehicles frequently disregard regulations and drive along tracks to overtake queuing traffic.

Because of the conflict with other traffic, the journey speeds of trams rarely exceed 12 kmph and are often as low as 8kmph. The Calcutta tramway for example is so delayed by traffic congestion, street trading and parking that, despite recent refurbishment of the system, the provincial government plans envisage its abandonment. The Cairo Tramway (Box 7.1) faces similar traffic problems, but upgrading has improved services. Nevertheless, like most tramways it continues to struggle to be viable.

TRAMWAY COSTS

Basic trams purchased recently, particularly from Eastern Europe, have cost as little as US $ 300,000 each. However, some cities have been encouraged by suppliers to purchase high technology trams costing in excess of US$ 1.5 million. New tracks and transmissions have cost in the region of US $ 4 million per km. To cover total costs, tram fares would need to be from 50 to 100 per cent higher than fares on conventional buses.

LRT METROS

While tramways may be losing popularity, LRT metros with their faster speeds and high capacity are attracting growing interest throughout the world. The distinguishing characteristics of LRT metros are that they comprise modern light rail vehicles, sometimes articulated, and are usually operated in trains. While parts of their networks may be along shared city streets, their tracks are generally completely segregated from other traffic either at grade, on viaducts or in underground tunnels (Table 7.2). The diversity of design options provides flexibility in coping with the different types of rights-of-way which may vary from one part of the city to the next. It also facilitates the staging of construction.

CAIRO TRAMS   BOX 7.1

Commuters in Cairo are provided with a wide variety of transport modes. By far the largest share of demand is supplied by buses with over 4 million passengers per day. This is followed by the regional metro which combines a short subway with the suburban railways and carries close to 1 million passengers per day. There is an extensive tramway network with a ridership of 300,000 passengers as well as an LRT with 200,000 daily passengers. There are also ferry services and over 14,000 shared taxis providing a significant alternative for commuters.

The Cairo Tramway, operated by the Cairo Transport Authority, has provided on-street services for commuters for close to 90 years. The system has a route length of 54km, half of which is segregated and half on-street. During the 1960s and until the late 1970s the quality of service was badly affected by traffic conditions and a lack of investment in rolling stock and infrastructure. A turning point was reached in 1977 when a start was made to progressively upgrade the system with improved tracks and power transmission, and modern rolling stock. The system now generally provides a better service in terms of both quantity and quality than in the past. However, trams are still delayed by other traffic where they do not enjoy exclusive rights of way. Overall average journey speeds are about 13kmph, slightly better than most tramways in Third World cities and reflecting the benefits of segregated tracks.

The Tramway operates some 250 cars formed into 2 or 3 car sets, spread over 16 routes. Headways on each route vary from 9 to 40 minutes. On sections where the concentration of routes is heaviest, trams operate at between 2 and 4 minute headways. Occupancy of trains is very low and even on the busiest routes, the two-car trains with a capacity of 326 passengers, rarely average more than 140, with a maximum of 260 during the peak period.

A flat fare of US 17 cents is charged throughout the network. Because of over-staffing, slow performance, low occupancy and the low fare, the Cairo Tramway makes a very substantial loss. With the current low level of earnings of passengers in Cairo, it is doubtful whether tram fares could ever be increased sufficiently to cover total costs. However, greater and more effective segregation of the tracks and other improvements, could be undertaken at comparatively low cost.

TABLE 7.2
Characteristics of selected Light Rail Transit Systems

City	Right-of-way:- elevated: elv under-ground: u/g at grade: a/g	Length km	Station spacing km	Minimum headway min:sec	Cars per train	Hourly design capacity p/h/d	Average journey speed kmph
Bogata	elevated	50.0	1.0	5.00	-	-	-
Hong Kong							
Tuen Mun	at grade	23.0	0.6	1.00	1/2	14,000	26
Istanbul	part u/g part a/g	24.0	1.3	1:30	3/4	28,000	-
Manila	elevated	14.0	1.2	2:00	2	25,000	28
Medellin	elevated	32.0	1.3	2:30	6	-	-
Mexico City							
Tren leger	part a/g part elv	11.0	-	-	-	-	-
Rio Line 2	part u/g part a/g	22.0	1.6	-	2	-	-
Tunis	at grade	10.0	0.8	1:00	2	24,000	19

Source: TRL Research Report 278

The interest in LRT metros has arisen because they are seen as providing higher levels of service compared to buses and trams, and at more affordable costs compared to full metros. Nevertheless the cost of LRT metros is still several times that of bus services, and as a result the interest in them has yet to be matched by investment. Currently there are less than 10 LRT metros in Third World cities. Most are comparatively short ranging from the 7km system of Istanbul to the 31km system of Tunis (Box 7.3). But for most LRT metros the sections in operation represent only the first phase of more extensive systems either planned or under construction, as in the case of Manila (Box 7.2)

MANILA LIGHT RAIL TRANSIT BOX 7.2

The Manila LRT, opened in 1985, is one of the most recently constructed systems in the Third World. It has proved to be very popular with users, cutting journey times from one hour to 30 minutes from end to end, and providing a smart and comfortable service which is generally reliable.

Metro Manila, the extensive urban area around Manila city, with a population of over 8 million has for many years suffered serious traffic problems. By far the majority of journeys in Manila are made in some 30,000 "Jeepneys" (paratransit vehicles derived from converted US Army surplus jeeps). They are fiercely competitive, and are virtually unregulated. Private car use, which is well above average for a Third World city, adds very significantly to traffic congestion. The construction of the LRT was seen as a means of not only providing a fast high capacity service for commuters but also as a means of reducing traffic congestion over the main commuter corridors.

The LRT is an elevated system running above the busy corridors from both the north and south into the centre of the city. The route, which currently consists of a single line with 18 stations, is 15km long. Rolling stock comprises 64 cars formed as 32 double articulated trains each with a crush capacity of 750 passengers. To cut capital and energy costs, cars are not air-conditioned and access to stations is by stairs rather than by escalators. While this is a distinct disadvantage, particularly during hot and humid weather, conditions for LRT passengers are far superior to those of commuters travelling by road transport.

The signalling and automatic train control system is designed to permit 1.5 minute headways. However, the peak headways actually operated are 2.5 minutes giving a line capacity of 18,000 passengers per hour per direction. Average patronage of the system is in the region of 270,000 passengers per day.

The total capital cost of the Manila LRT has been estimated at US$ 563 million (1986 prices). While the annual revenue at US$13.0 million exceeds operation costs, when depreciation and interest are taken into account the system runs at a loss in excess of US$3 million per year. Increased capacity and extension of the system is planned but will depend on suitable funding being obtained.

The system is owned by the Light Rail Transit Authority, a government corporation, and is operated and maintained by Metro Inc. under a ten year contract. Metro Inc. is a subsidiary of the private sector power supply company, The Manila Electric Railway and Light Company. This arrangement has proved to be somewhat unsatisfactory and alternative options are under consideration.

The Manila LRT has clearly achieved the objective of providing superior means of transport for commuters. However, although there were initial improvements to road traffic after the opening of the LRT, these have not been sustained. In some places along the route traffic conditions are worse than ever due to a) the narrowing of roads to accommodate the LRT structure, b) a rise in disorderly loading and unloading by jeepneys and c) obstruction caused by street vendors attracted to the streets around LRT stations and terminals.

LRT metros usually comprise 4, 6, or 8 axle articulated cars operating singly or in sets of 2 or 3 cars. The capacity of cars is between 100 and 375 passengers each. Almost without exception, LRT metros are powered by 750V dc over head transmission systems.

A typical LRT train consisting of three double-articulated units has a crush capacity of up to 800-900 passengers. On exclusive tracks with grade separated intersections, journey speeds, including stops, are 15-25 kmph. Peak capacity is between 20,000 and 30,000 passengers per hour per track. (Flows of 36,000 have been claimed. However there is little evidence to suggest that this can be achieved on a day to day basis even on completely exclusive tracks)

Where intersections are not grade separated considerable problems arise. To maintain high capacity at grade, LRT vehicles have to be given a measure of priority, and with almost a continuous flow of LRT vehicles across intersections crossing and turning traffic is seriously disrupted. This particular problem has arisen in Tunis where costly tunnelling appears to be the planned solution (Box 7.3).

When constructed at ground level, a light rail infrastructure composed of trackway, signals, and power system will cost between US$6 million and US$10 million per km. Elevated systems can be expected to cost between US$25 million and US$40 million per km, while underground sections may cost almost as much as full metros. The cost of light rail vehicles in 1985 was approximately US$800,000 each. Total costs for well run and patronised surface LRTs with exclusive rights of way are in the region of 10 US cents to 15 US cents/passenger km.

Generally, light rail systems are confined to main traffic corridors and are not suitable for distributing passengers throughout secondary and tertiary road networks. The consequent need for many passengers to change modes during their journeys is a distinct disadvantage of light rail systems. Bus services, by comparison, as well as being more affordable, serve the entire road network and can be routed to greatly reduce the need for passengers to interchange between services.

Some authorities, while recognising that LRT metros may not be justified in their cities for some time, are prudently keeping their options open. In Addis Ababa, for example, town plans make provision for the right-of-way of a future LRT, to be constructed when justified by increased demand and level of earnings. In the case of Karachi, busways are being designed to be readily converted to LRT in the future when similarly justified. The earlier provision of LRT in Karachi could take place in response to aspirations of an improved image for the city.

TUNIS LIGHT RAIL TRANSIT   BOX 7.3

Tunis, with a population of 1.5 million has developed around two large lakes with the city centre squeezed between them. Commuter traffic is thus concentrated into a few narrow corridors and with rapid growth in demand, traffic congestion has become a serious problem. In particular, congestion has substantially reduced the operating speed and reliability of buses. In the face of this situation a decision was made to enhance the public transport system by replacing buses with a light rail system along major commuter corridors. Bus services, with over 750,000 passengers per day, continue to be the major mode of traffic for the city as a whole.

The Tunis LRT comprises four radial lines each leading to the city centre. The system has 36 stations closely spaced at 700 meters and a total route length of 25 km. The tracks, which are all currently at ground level, wend their way, sometimes tortuously and slowly, along existing streets. They are fully segregated except at road crossings where the trains are given priority by means of traffic signals.

The trains are operated in sets of two double articulated cars, with overhead power supply of 750V dc. Each car carries 364 passengers. Peak headways are between 4-6 minutes, and with the completion of further stages of the system in mid-1990, ridership increased from 75,000 passengers a day in 1989 to over 170,000 per day.

Because of frequent trains creating a virtual barrier, there is considerable potential for serious disruption to cross city traffic, business activities and pedestrians. This applies particularly to a section of about 600 meters through the heart of the city, which has been the subject of considerable controversy. As a result plans have been formulated to place the offending section underground adding very substantially to the cost of the system.

Capital costs up to November 1990, which excludes the proposed tunnel, are estimated at US$200 million. Projected total capital costs for the 32km system, including the proposed tunnel and a 7km extension under construction, are estimated to be US$240 million. Because fares are held artificially low to reduce competition from buses, revenue is unable to cover even basic operating costs. As a result the LRT receives large capital and operating subsidies.

The Tunis LRT has not achieved any reduction in road congestion and in some places has exacerbated conditions for other road users. However, it has clearly met its primary objectives of providing a more reliable, regular and faster service than previously provided by buses. While it has attracted few motorists, it has proved to be very popular with most other commuters. Mainly because of the comparatively high level of earnings in Tunis and the appreciable journey time savings, the Tunis LRT shows a satisfactory economic return.

8 SUBURBAN RAILWAYS

A number of cities in the Third World make use of heavy railways to provide their suburbs or close-by urban areas with commuter services (Plate 8.1). Most of these services share the tracks and stations with inter-city freight and passenger trains, and in some cases, use similar rolling stock. A few enjoy substantial patronage,; for example, the Western and Central railways of Bombay between them carry over 5 million commuters each day. The Calcutta Eastern railway carries over 1 million passengers per day, while suburban heavy rail services in Sao Paulo, Rio de Janeiro, Cairo and Madras, each carry in the region of 0.5 to 1 million passengers daily (Table 8.1).

Several systems, because they are not aligned close enough to high demand areas, or do not terminate conveniently near city centres, are poorly patronized. Examples at the lower end of the scale are the Karachi and Lagos commuter rail services which each carry in the region of only 7000 and 15000 passengers per day respectively. In Karachi the railway skirts the heavy demand corridors and is not appropriate for commuter traffic. In the case of Lagos, one particular factor which greatly reduces the value of the railway as a commuter service is the termination of the railway on the mainland before reaching the central business district located on Lagos Island. It is estimated that the CBD together with many government offices on Lagos Island generates over 1.5 million passenger trips each day. These are mainly met by buses using the three road bridges connecting with Lagos Island. In sharp contrast the suburban rail system in Bombay is very well located which accounts for its massive patronage (Box 8.1).

The rolling stock of suburban railways generally comprises electrical multiple units in 3 or 4 sets, or in larger sets of 8 or 9 cars. Some comprise conventional heavy rail carriages hauled by diesel

TABLE 8.1
Suburban railways: major systems

City	Length km	Lines (main)	Annual passenger trips (millions)
Bombay, Western	94	3	750
Bombay, Central	64	4	736
Calcutta	446	8	380
Sao Paulo, CBTU	190	2	220
Sao Paulo, FEPASA	64	2	102
Rio de Janeiro	370	10	182
Hong Kong, KCR	34	1	171
Cairo	33	2	160
Madras	115	3	143
Istanbul	70	2	90

Source: Author's research and Jane's Urban Transport Systems 1991

Plate 8.1a   Suburban trains run parallel with line 2 of the metro system, Rio de Janeiro

Plate 8.1b   A suburban train in Lagos, Nigeria

BOMBAY SUBURBAN RAILWAYS   BOX 8.1

By far the most extensively used network of suburban rail services in the Third World is found in Metropolitan Bombay (over 4000 sq km; population 11 million). The Western Railway and Central Railway, divisions of the Indian Railways, between them carry more than 5 million commuters each day. A similar number is carried on bus services largely operated by BEST (Bombay Electric Supply and Transport Undertaking). While the majority of commuters reside within Greater Bombay (438 sq km; population 9 million), the suburban railways serve the very extensive Bombay Metropolitan Region . Very long journeys to and from work are a way of life for a high proportion of commuters in Bombay. Average suburban rail trips are particularly long at 24km - almost four times average bus trips.

The Western Railway operates two parallel routes passing through the central area. One between Churchgate in the south and Virar in the north, a distance of 60 km, and one between Churchgate and Borivali near the boundary of Greater Bombay, a distance of 34 km. Some of the tracks in the central area are for the exclusive use of suburban trains, but on the fast commuter corridor between Bombay Central and Virar, suburban trains share the tracks with long distance trains. The Western Railway currently operates about 60 nine-car EMUs at frequencies of 4 minutes during the peak and 17 minutes off-peak. Altogether, the Western Railway runs over 800 scheduled suburban services each day and serves 53 stations.

The Central Railway serves 28 stations and runs over 1000 suburban services daily. These are provided along three routes out of Victoria Terminus, in the city centre, using 100 trains mainly comprising 9 car EMUs. Two routes run the 54km to Thane with a peak headway of 5 minutes. The other route is a harbour link to Bandra and Anderi with a headway of about 15 minutes. There are a number of branch lines, including a link to the Western Railway. Like the Western Railway, some of the routes are for the exclusive use of suburban trains but others are shared with long distance and freight trains. The services are mainly electrified and are powered by 1.5kV dc. Some of the trains are hauled by diesel locomotives. Both systems use automatic block signalling.

The suburban railways in Bombay are extremely heavily loaded with trains designed for a crush loading of 1728 passengers, regularly carrying in excess of 3000 passengers during peak periods. The fare for an average 25 km trip is Rupees 3.00 (US 15 cents), which is equivalent to less than US 1.00 cent per km. However, most commuters pay even less by making use of monthly season tickets which are

locomotives. Capacity of systems varies very considerably and depends on train size and frequency, and delays that may be caused by inter-city express trains and freight trains. A typical suburban railway comprising eight-car trains carries 2400 passengers per train. Efficient systems on shared tracks handle 10,000 to 20,000 passengers per hour in one direction. On exclusive tracks, capacity may exceed the maximum for LRT.

Most systems are based on long established railways with wide ranging cost differences. Systems which recently have been upgraded and electrified making use of existing rights of way have been found to involve capital costs as low as US$2-5 million per km for infrastructure and equipment and US$1 million for each car. Therefore, providing an existing railway is well located for commuters, its upgrading to a fast and high capacity system is likely to show good returns. Financial and economic viability may, however, be elusive where upgrading is costly and earnings are low. In Jakarta, for example, upgrading of the heavy railway involves very substantial and costly grade separation mainly because of the large number of existing level crossings. Also the existing alignment does not serve the city centre and the construction of an expensive new inner city loop is required. The high cost of upgrading and the low level of earnings in Jakarta, reduces the chances of either financial or economic viability.

Such problems have not arisen with the upgrading of the Kowloon-Canton Railway in Hong Kong. Full use has been made of the original right-of-way which was mainly grade-separated and which serves a corridor of very high demand. As a result upgrading costs were comparatively low. Furthermore, the earnings of users are high (more than ten times the level in Jakarta). The work involved modernisation, double tracking and electrification to provide fast and convenient commuter services between the very high density urban area of Kowloon and the rapidly expanding new towns close by. The metro-type commuter trains share the tracks with heavy rail inter-city passenger and freight trains. The system, which carries in excess of 500,000 passengers daily, is financially viable and achieves a high economic rate of return.

9 TRAFFIC MANAGEMENT: IMPACT ON PUBLIC TRANSPORT

Most cities in the Third World suffer from heavy traffic congestion and frequent traffic accidents. They face all the traffic problems found in industrialised countries - insufficient road capacity, on-street parking and vehicle loading, many uneconomic road users, conflicting traffic movements, and heavy through traffic. In addition they often have to contend with much on-street trading, many hand-drawn and animal drawn vehicles, poor road surface conditions, many broken-down vehicles and considerable lack of regard for traffic regulations. Under these circumstances, together with the rapid growth of traffic and a general lack of resources, city authorities find it difficult to escape a worsening situation. Often the most seriously affected are buses and minibuses, which in Third World countries account for the great majority of passenger trips.

There is strong pressure to approach these problems through the construction of extensive and politically attractive new transport infrastructures. However, few developing countries can afford these costly solutions. Although many may lack the political will to undertake less attractive solutions, cities are increasingly turning to more cost effective alternatives. In particular traffic management is becoming more recognised as a very effective means of reducing congestion and improving the flow of public transport. While the physical works involved are often well within the scope of local skills, planning and design calls for specialist training which is often lacking but which can be readily obtained. However, although more and more traffic management schemes are being tried, by far the greatest stumbling block to success has been the absence of effective enforcement of traffic regulations. In addition, as most schemes are designed to favour public transport, they are often up against stiff opposition from motorists who generally comprise the most influential group in any society.

Despite the difficulties of introducing and enforcing traffic management measures, there have been a large number of reasonably effective schemes. Although some may not have fully lived up to expectations, they have nevertheless generally provided worthwhile benefits with high economic rates of return. In fact more than a few have achieved outstanding success. Some of these have concentrated on particular trouble spots, such as the centres of major cities; for example, in Karachi where successful gyratory and tidal flow systems have been introduced. Others have involved comprehensive traffic management measures and road improvement schemes embracing a large part of the city, as in the case of the very successful approach in Abidjan, in the Cote d'Ivoire (Box 9.1).

The need for traffic management to give particular attention to public transport is well recognised and the value of priority measures for buses (and to a lesser extent minibuses) is acknowledged by most authorities. In some cases however, measures have unintentionally had an adverse effect on buses, or because of pressure have favoured motorists. In Seoul, to improve traffic flow along a major commuting corridor, an elevated express-way has been constructed for the exclusive use of private cars. As a result, more economic road users, such as buses and trucks, are jammed into

ABIDJAN: COMPREHENSIVE TRAFFIC MANAGEMENT   BOX 9.1

Faced with serious traffic problems, typical of many Third World cities, the government of Cote d'Ivoire undertook comprehensive, low-cost traffic management and road improvement schemes throughout Abidjan, the capital. Key sections of the city's road network had been badly overloaded, with congestion in the CBD lasting for much of the day. In many parts of the city, buses, taxis, trucks, cars and pedestrians competed for the limited road space which was frequently reduced by parked cars and street traders. As the population and motorisation grew, congestion became more acute and widespread. Transport costs soared and bus services, in particular, were often reduced to a crawl.

The integrated measures taken to combat this situation emphasised the needs of public transport and included the provision of:

-     a system of one-way streets, traffic signs and road markings,
-     136 sets of traffic signals controlled by computer,
-     footbridges for the movement and safety of pedestrians,
-     the provision of a busway and reserved bus lanes in the CBD,
-     new road links, particularly for a high-speed express bus network,
-     facilities for buses, comprising depots, terminals and bus stops,
-     a traffic management unit and a transport studies group, and
-     effective steps to improve the enforcement of traffic and street trading regulations.

The results of these measures, which were mainly undertaken with the assistance of the World Bank, were considerable improvements throughout the city. Amongst the most important outcomes were the reduction of the journey times by half for buses crossing the CBD and the enhancement of bus services and traffic conditions generally.

Major contributions to the success of the schemes have been the effective enforcement of traffic regulations by the Traffic Police and the efficient day-to-day management of the traffic system by the Traffic Management Unit.

---

the limited road space below the express-way (Plate 9.1). Fortunately schemes such as this are the exception, and there is now a growing tendency to provide effective priority to public transport. As well as busways, described in Chapter 5, priority measures mainly comprise "with-flow" and "contra-flow" bus or tram only lanes. Other devices sometimes used include "bus and tram-only" cross traffic turning movements and the provision of priority for buses and trams at traffic signals. Despite opposition from motorists, these schemes often provide benefits for all road users - private cars and commercial vehicles, as well as buses and trams. In some cases, without reducing general traffic speeds, reserved bus lanes have permitted bus journey speeds to be increased, often to more than 20 kmph. Passenger volumes of about 15000 passengers per hour per lane for standard buses and 20000 passengers per hour per lane for larger buses have been achieved. However, these very good results are dependant on good enforcement. Generally the effectiveness of bus-only lanes has been very mixed.

With-flow bus only lanes in the Third World (or for that matter, throughout the world) have received only limited success. This is due to the ease with which other vehicles are able to encroach into these lanes and to evade prosecution. As a result enforcement, which needs to be

Plate 9.1   Expressway for cars in Seoul, South Korea: buses remain locked in the congested road below

constant, is difficult and often neglected. Notable success have been achieved by "with flow" bus-only lanes in Bangkok, but over time a softening of enforcement has lead to a reduction of their effectiveness. (See Bangkok Bus Only Lanes: Box 9.2 and Plate 9.2)

Contra-flow bus-only lanes generally have achieved better results. They are to a certain extent self-enforcing. Encroachment by other vehicles is far more difficult and hazardous, and as a result is not so frequent as with "with-flow" bus-only lanes. One disadvantage sometimes experienced with contra-flow bus-only lanes is that pedestrians not expecting to see buses approaching from the opposite direction to the main traffic flow are taken by surprise. For example, the introduction of contra flow trolleybus-only lanes in Rio de Janeiro led initially to an increase in pedestrian accidents.

The difficulties with both types of bus lane have led to the provision of segregation devices, such as high kerbs or fences, and to the evolution of exclusive busways.

ROAD PRICING AND USER RESTRAINTS

Many countries have considered the use of road pricing and car user restraints as a means of reducing road congestion and to improve, in particular, conditions for public transport. Several different systems of restraint are used or at least have been attempted in developing countries.

BANGKOK: BUS-ONLY LANES   BOX 9.2

Bangkok is one of the busiest cities in the Third World. It is also one of the most congested. Although the city is reasonably well served by major radial highways, it lacks suitable secondary roads and access roads, precluding efficient use of the road system as a whole. The shortage of these roads forces local traffic to use the main roads and results in long needless detours, making journey speeds slow and vehicle operating costs high.

Over two-thirds of motorized passenger trips in Bangkok are made by public transport which comprises some 5000 standard buses and 5000 minibuses. The Thai Government have thus approached the problem by implementing a traffic management project that emphasises priority for buses and minibuses. The project, undertaken with the support of the World Bank, comprised an urban traffic control system, a series of comprehensive route and junction improvement schemes and an extensive 145km network of bus priority lanes, later to be increased to 200 km.

Prior to implementation of the project, the speed of trips during peak periods in the central area was as low as 10 kmph, while cars were able to maintain only little better than 12 kmph. Surveys carried out subsequently showed that as a result of the comprehensive measures, both bus and car travel times had improved significantly in almost all cases providing substantial economic benefits in terms of time and fuel savings. In areas where the most success was achieved, buses and cars mean travel speeds were increased by 25 to 30 per cent. On none of the streets surveyed did bus or car travel times worsen. That cars did not suffer as a result of priority given for buses has been attributed to the more orderly manoeuvring of vehicles.

Observed bus flows were very high, with up to 250 standard buses and 150 private minibuses using a single bus lane during an average peak hour. In total these vehicles had a carrying capacity of about 18000 passengers per hour.

Follow-up surveys showed further improvements to bus and car travel times. Subsequently however, police enforcement waned and bus lane violations increased, so that some of the benefits were badly eroded. Furthermore, the introduction of a one-way system in central Bangkok, which did appear to raise journey speeds within the system, created very large queues of vehicles at the entry points to the system. As a result, overall journey times within the city deteriorated.

AREA LICENSING SCHEMES

Considerable interest has been shown in the Singapore Area Licensing Scheme (See Box 9.3 and Plate 9.3), in which vehicles are charged for entering or operating in a certain area through a system of permits. Efficient users of road space, ie high occupancy vehicles and commercial vehicles, may be exempt. The system is applied to congested areas during peak periods. It encourages greater use of public transport and shared private cars and discourages unnecessary journeys. However, the introduction of area licensing schemes, when tried in Bangkok and Kuala Lumpur, proved to be politically, and to some extent technically, difficult, and had to be abandoned.

Plate 9.2 *Priority lane for buses: Bangkok, Thailand*

ELECTRONIC ROAD PRICING

A more sophisticated approach, electronic road pricing, involves placing electronic number plates on vehicles and recording their passage over loops in the road surface placed at strategic locations in the road network. A variation involves in-vehicle meters into which priced units can be stored. As the vehicle passes a loop or transmitter, units are used up. In this way motorists are charged for their actual use of the road. Charges may be fixed or related to the degree of congestion. Electronic road pricing proved to be technically and economically feasible in a pilot scheme in Hong Kong, but was rejected on social and political grounds. The cost and level of technology is high and may not be feasible in low income cities. Nevertheless the system is very promising and variations of the Hong Kong system may be more acceptable.

MOVEMENT RESTRICTIONS

In some places road user restraints have been applied by restricting cross city movements by private cars. For example, a beneficial reduction of traffic flow has been achieved in Tunis by dividing the central business district into "cells." Public transport and emergency vehicles are allowed to cross the borders between cells, but other traffic must use entrances and exits onto routes that bypass the central area. The completed first phase of the scheme has produced promising results and extensions are under consideration. The cost of providing the necessary additional capacity on bypass routes in the future, together with additional fuel consumption

SINGAPORE AREA LICENSING SCHEME   BOX 9.3

Singapore was the first, and for many years the only, country in the world effectively to use private car restraints as a means of combating central area traffic problems. Its unique Area Licensing Scheme (ALS), introduced in 1975, has shown that with a firm government commitment, a well planned package of restraints, coupled with public transport and road improvements, can significantly reduce city centre congestion.

The scheme has been modified in recent years but the original arrangements have well withstood the test of time. Initially the scheme involved the application of a charge to low-occupancy vehicles entering the central business district during the morning rush period (7:30 to 10:15). A cordon around the central business district demarcates the restricted area with vehicles able to enter only at clearly marked entry points. Low-occupancy private cars were, and still are, required to display a special area license disk for which a fee is charged (initially US$ 2.50 a day or US$ 50 per month). For most of the life of the scheme private cars with four or more occupants, goods vehicles and buses were exempt from paying the fee. The fees were increased from time to time and have been as high as US$ 5.00 a day or US$ 100 per month.

Included in the scheme has been the provision of inexpensive car parks to allow motorists to park at the periphery of the licensed area, with shuttle buses to transport them to the city centre. Parking charges within the restricted area were raised substantially to further discourage the use of private cars. To restrain the rapid growth in ownership of private cars, high annual license fees were introduced. An important part of the scheme has been the provision of alternative routes for through traffic. Strict enforcement of the rules against illegal parking, combined with a large degree of public acceptance of the scheme has lead to a low incidence of offences against the scheme. However, the park-and-ride arrangements proved to be unpopular with motorists and were curtailed and the shuttle buses diverted to routes to carry passengers directly from residential areas to the city centre.

The scheme resulted in a dramatic and sustained decrease in traffic congestion during the morning rush hour and greater use of public transport. Fears that the scheme might adversely affect business and other activities have generally not been substantiated. Any impact that the scheme may have had on land values, land use and the environment have been largely eclipsed by other factors.

It had been expected that the reduction of commuting by private car would also reduce congestion during the evening peak period, but apart from some initial improvement, this has not been so. In fact, over the years congestion in the evening has become much worse. This has been attributed to greater use of private cars for afternoon shopping and for collecting school children and office workers. There has also been evidence of many commercial vehicles using the central area as a short cut. As a result, in 1989 the Government extended the ALS to include the evening rush period and to apply charges to all vehicles except authorised buses. The rate for private cars was reduced to US$ 3.00 per day with the same rate of US$ 3.00 also applied to taxis and most other vehicles. The exceptions are company cars which are now charged US$ 6.00 and motorcycles US$ 1.00 per day. There have been suggestions of an adverse impact on afternoon shopping in the central area. But the changes have proved to be very effective in reducing traffic congestion and add significantly to the benefits that the scheme has accrued since it was introduced in 1975.

Plate 9.3   Gantry indicating the start of the area licensing zone in Singapore: buses are exempt

costs due to more circuitous journeys, may be considerable and are being carefully weighed against the benefits of reduced congestion and traffic accidents in the city centre.

PARKING CONTROLS

Many countries have introduced parking charges and controls to overcome parking problems. However, few have yet to follow the example of Singapore, where parking controls are designed specifically to restrain the use of private cars in congested areas at peak periods and encourage the use of buses. Here, controls are applied and charges set to discourage commuters. But to avoid an adverse effect on traders and shoppers, reduced rates apply during off-peak periods. As a means of restraint, parking controls are less sophisticated and less costly than other measures, and are therefore very appropriate for use in Third World cities. Furthermore where parking controls already exist, rigorous application can provide a comparatively easy first step in a restraint programme. Such an approach to restraint is planned and is already being pursued in a number of Third World cities, including for example Karachi, Jakarta and Abidjan.

NUMBER PLATE RESTRICTIONS

In Lagos direct restraint is applied to motor cars by restricting their use to alternate days of the week: cars with even number plates one day, and odd number plates the next. The scheme was introduced to deal with the chronic traffic congestion experienced in Lagos, and was designed to cut in half the flow of traffic to and from Lagos island. However, the effectiveness of this system has been greatly eroded by the increase in the number of two-car families (or two-number plate families), and many vehicles, such as government cars, being exempt from the restrictions.

VEHICLE AND FUEL CHARGES AND TAXES

In many countries the low level of earning and the sheer cost of purchasing and running vehicles are very considerable restraints on ownership and use. High costs result from high import duties, sales tax, licensing fees, and fuel tax. Usually these are seen as a means of raising revenue and reducing the drain on foreign exchange, rather than a means of traffic control. In only a few places is the policy to impose taxes for traffic reasons; examples are Hong Kong and Seoul where the aim was also to encourage greater use of public transport. In Hong Kong the results were very effective, with the rate of growth in vehicle numbers held down for many years. In Seoul, high acquisition taxes, including bonds for the metro, high annual licence fees and particularly high fuel tax, result in the country having one of the lowest ratios of cars to population despite the high level of earnings.

10 FARES AND FARE COLLECTION

FARE REGULATION

In most Third World countries, public transport fares are controlled by government. Generally the way in which fares are regulated is based on political rather than financial or economic considerations, with authorities under pressure to keep fares down despite rising costs. This pressure is particularly acute where controlled fare schedules apply nationwide, so that any fare increase becomes a national issue. In the case of most public undertakings, resistance to fare increases adds significantly to losses and the need for heavy subsidies.

While some private sector operators, when faced with regulated fares that do not keep pace with rising costs, may, in severe cases, go out of business, most seem able to survive. They do this by adopting a variety of measures to increase revenue and reduce costs. Where the enforcement of fares is lax or difficult, some form of overcharging or supplementary charging is widely practised. Apart from simply demanding higher fares from passengers, operators may for example, charge the regulated fares but apply these to shortened routes, or to part of a scheduled route. They may also supplement takings by charging for the carriage of passengers' goods including even small belongings, since these usually are not covered by regulations. In some places, drivers' assistants have been seen "helping" passengers to board buses or to change money for a "helpers fee" to supplement revenue. For example in Onitsha, Nigeria, it is difficult to board a bus without "help", while in Monrovia, Liberia, "helpers" charge 10 cents for changing a dollar! (Plate 10.1).

Operators take steps to reduce costs by successive lowering of standards, skimping on maintenance and repairs, and by making no specific provision for replacements.

While the intention of keeping fares down may be to protect the interest of the public, in practice the effects are often to the long term detriment of services. Inevitably, as returns dwindle, investment dries up and the quantity and quality of services decline. It is clearly evident in Third World cities from the considerable use of shared taxis that many passengers are prepared to pay more for more convenient and comfortable services. (In most cities shared taxi fares are often several times more than bus fares for the same distance).

In some places, the importance of ensuring that services are viable is recognised, and fares, although controlled are in some way indexed to costs or inflation. For example, authorities in Montevideo have created a bus operating cost index as a basis for regular fare revisions. These normally take place about every 4 months and being in small increments are accepted by the public with comparative ease.

There is a growing trend towards more flexibility in the regulation of fares, but this usually extends only to premium services such as all-seater buses, coach and express services. Although the advantages of unregulated fares coupled with free competition are often well recognised by

Plate 10.1   'Helpers' giving change for a fee: minibuses in Monrovia, Liberia

government finance ministry staff, in very few places do operators legally have freedom to determine the fares that they charge. Fares and access to the market are unregulated in Colombo and as a result of fierce competition, operators keep fares as low as US 7 cents for a 5km trip.

In the few places where private operators are able to decide on the level of fares, the public are likely to be overcharged if access to the market is restricted and there is no effective competition to keep prices down. This applies particularly where unions have strong control and virtually create a monopoly as in the case of Guatemala City where there are plenty of buses but unions force up fares. Competition is also restricted where public transport systems are state monopolies. However, under these circumstances fares usually are controlled, and held down by the provision of subsidies, so the question of overcharging does not arise.

FARE SYSTEMS

Flat fares, (ie fares that are the same for any journey within the city, regardless of distance or zones), apply widely throughout the Third World. Often there are reductions for different classes of passengers (eg children and students) and variations for different types of vehicle (eg coaches, and minibuses). Flat fares are favoured, particularly by public corporations, because of the ease of collection and control. However, government planners generally concede that flat fares have

71

Plate 10.2   Excessive interchange resulting from fares control, Lagos, Nigeria

several drawbacks. In particular, they are inclined to encourage longer journeys, and thus run counter to the aim of town plans that foster balanced development and minimise transport needs. Also, in order to boost revenue, there is a tendency for operators to reduce the length of bus routes so that many users are forced to change buses during their journeys and pay more than one fare, for example, in Lagos (Plate 10.2). In other places where flat fares are imposed by regulation, operators are reluctant to serve areas some distance from city centres. These anomalies are found throughout the Third World. Typical are the reduction of route lengths by the public corporation in Addis Ababa and the introduction of unnecessary interchanges midway in journeys by private operators in Medelin, Colombia. Both devices are designed to optimise revenue and clearly circumvent flat fare regulations.

Distance-based fares, while being more difficult to collect and control, are nonetheless found mainly in the larger cities. Being more closely related to costs, they are acknowledged as overcoming the disadvantages of flat fares by encouraging more economic travel patterns, with long term benefits for city development. Examples of well graduated fares are in Bombay, Calcutta, Karachi and Shanghai. Clearly the perceived collection problems of distance based fares have been overcome in these cities.

Zonal fares provide a popular compromise to overcome the drawbacks of flat and distance based fares. In this system, urban areas are divided into zones and different fares are charged for

72

travelling within zones and from one zone to another. Zonal fares are comparatively easy to collect and understand, and incorporate some relationship of costs to distance, particularly in the case of longer journeys. A typical zonal system applies in Nairobi whereby flat fares of US 15 cents are charged within zones, and excess fares of US 5 cents are charged for each zone crossed.

Season tickets, multiple trip tickets and passes, are comparatively rare except in India. Because of the outlay required of passengers, they usually are found only in medium and high income countries.

FARE COLLECTION METHODS

With very few exceptions, bus fares in developing countries are collected by conductors travelling with the buses. Drivers may also assist with the collection of fares, but rarely are buses one-man-operated (Plate 10.3). With low income levels and underemployment, labour costs generally are not a significant factor in bus operations in most Third World cities. As a result, even on small buses and minibuses, the crews often consist of at least one conductor. In the case of small paratransit vehicles, such as auto-rickshaws and the like, fares are collected by the driver.

To reduce revenue losses, most public bus and rail corporations and some of the larger private companies issue tickets. In the case of owner-operated or small family enterprises, fare collectors are usually trusted family members or close colleagues and there is little need to use tickets to keep a check on fares paid.

Turnstiles and hand held ticket printing machines are used on buses in a number of countries. In Brazil many public and private buses utilize turnstiles with built-in counters. The turnstile on each bus is operated by the collector, who is able to block the entry of passengers into the main body of the bus until they have paid their fares. To reduce boarding delays, the rear entry platform is large enough to accommodate about twenty passengers waiting to go through the turnstile.

Prepaid tickets purchased at stations are the most common method used by urban railways, with some of the more advanced systems using automatic ticket dispensing machines. However, because of their high cost and level of technology involved, automatic ticket dispensing machines for bus services are found in very few places. Sao Paulo is a rare exception. Its state of the art busway system uses magnetic strip tickets sold at automatic booths on platforms. The tickets are inserted into turnstiles on the buses to gain access. Plans exist to integrate this ticketing system with the metro. Also in Sao Paulo, the bus operators association sells prepaid tokens to employers who pass these on to their employees, sometimes at a discount.

A novel system to reduce revenue losses has been introduced in Lima, Peru. In this system bus tickets are also raffle tickets. Raffles are held monthly and winners receive handsome prizes. Passengers now insist on being given tickets, which they carefully retain. Apart from an increase in the number of passengers paying the correct fare, the records of fare collection have become more reliable and the opportunities for fraud have been reduced.

Plate 10.3   Simple arrangements operated by driver and conductor for controlling passenger boarding and alighting: Delhi Transport Corporation

11 FINANCING PUBLIC TRANSPORT

Raising funds to maintain satisfactory public transport services is thwart with difficulties, particularly so in the Third World. The lack of funds is, with few exceptions, the primary reason why services are so frequently inadequate in both quality and quantity. In the case of bus services, public sector operators generally run at a substantial loss and have to rely heavily on subsidies. With growing demand and rising costs they are in constant need of larger and larger subsidies, which rarely if ever become available in full. While private operators are generally financially viable, they frequently face difficulties in raising funds, particularly the foreign exchange elements for spares and new vehicles. Because of larger deficits and much higher capital costs, the funding of rail systems faces even greater difficulties.

The lack of funding for urban transport stems mainly from a number of inter-related factors:

- the low income of users,
- the stagnation of national economies,
- severe cutbacks of public spending,
- stiff competition between sectors,
- steep growth in outstanding debts, and
- decline in both official and private lending.

Because of the difficulty of raising public funds, Third World governments are turning more and more to the private sector to finance urban transport, while still relying heavily on international and bilateral assistance.

Sources and extent of funding available for public transport vary considerably from country to country, but generally include:

- direct income: mainly fare box revenue,
- government grants in the form of operating and capital subsidies,
- development income, from buildings at stations for example,
- hypothecated revenue (revenue earmarked to fund specific services),
- commercial loans,
- suppliers credits,
- international and bilateral grants and loans, and
- private investment, including "build operate and transfer" (BOT) and joint ventures.

The funding of a system may often comprise several of these sources. In the case of large capital intensive projects, such as metros, comprehensive packages of funding devices are usually employed.

FUNDING BY USERS - FARE BOX REVENUE

All public transport operators rely to a varying extent on funding by direct income, which is mainly in the form of fare box revenue but sometimes includes small amounts of income from advertising and contract work. When direct income does not cover costs, it is usually supplemented by subsidies, though some operators have to resort to other means (for example, non-payment of taxes, delaying payments to staff and creditors, non-provision for depreciation).

Very few public sector bus or rail services, if any, are able to rely entirely on direct revenue. An examination by the World Bank of 20 representative public sector bus operators revealed that on average only 62 per cent of total costs (operating costs, depreciation and interest) was recovered from fare box revenue and other direct income. For urban railways the figure is even lower and generally in the region of 30 per cent.

Public corporations often are expected to at least recover operating costs from users, but few are successful with this aim. Exceptions are, for example, the Hong Kong metro and a number of well run Indian bus corporations which are able to cover not only operating costs, including depreciation, but also are able to make a useful contribution to interest charges.

Public corporations may give the impression of dominating public transport, but in practice, by far the greatest proportion of public transport trips in the Third World are made in private sector bus and minibus services. Almost all of these are able to survive on fare box revenue alone. Thus by far the majority of services are funded solely by users. An examination by the World Bank of 33 large representative cities found that fare box revenue was, in effect, the sole source of funding for over 75 per cent of bus and minibus trips. In addition, there are vast fleets of shared taxis and other forms of paratransit vehicles, which similarly are self-supporting. In the case of medium and small cities, an even higher proportion of users pay the full cost of their trips. In these cities the availability of public corporation services is generally less, and the prevalence of private sector operators much greater than in the larger cities.

The funding of bus services solely by users is only possible because costs are low and because the majority of users accept a low standard of comfort and safety. Those prepared to pay more tend towards the use of private cars or paratransit rather than towards subsidized services which are rarely any better than self-supporting services.

Although many services are able to survive solely on fare box revenue, it is a matter for conjecture whether or not these are financially sound. Few make any formal provision for depreciation, and probably even fewer carry any insurance: almost all profess to have been making a loss for years. Under these circumstances, it would be reasonable to expect bus and minibus fleets to be in a steep decline. However, in the majority of cities, the reverse is more the case with private sector operators thriving and expanding without subsidies and with very little other assistance. Fairly typical is Calcutta where, despite very low fares, the private sector bus and minibus fleets have expanded steadily from about 2000 in 1980 to well over 3000 in 1990. In only a few places are private bus and minibus fleets declining. Usually this is due to factors in addition to low farebox revenue. For example, in the case of Lagos, most operators seem able to overcome fare regulations and cover normal costs. However, they have been unable to replace ageing vehicles because of a 10-fold increase over five years in the cost of vehicles and spares due to the realignment of the local currency exchange rate. As a result between 1983 and 1988 private bus fleets declined from 18000 to 10000. In Karachi, where private buses also rely entirely on fare box revenue, artificially held down fares and a ban on the licensing of replacement or new minibuses resulted in the fleet of buses and minibuses falling from 6000 in 1986 to 4000 in 1990. Such declines in private sector fleets relying on fare box revenue are very much the exception. Most are expanding despite operators' apparent lack of provision for replacements and claims of financial hardship.

SUBSIDIES

As mentioned above, most public sector bus and rail operators rely heavily on both operating and capital subsidies. Very few private operators receive direct subsidies but may benefit from infrastructure provided at below cost or at no cost. In some places subsidies are applied directly to certain types of passengers, for example, in the form of concessionary fares for students.

Subsidies are normally provided by national, state or city governments, usually from general revenue, but in some cases from hypothecated revenue such as road taxes raised from vehicle licensing or fuel tax. A novel arrangement in Korea requires all vehicle purchasers to buy zero-interest bonds in the metros. In Seoul, the bonds, which are repayable in five years are set at US$1000. Revenue from these bonds is estimated to cover 15 per cent of the cost of the metro.

Governments generally fund subsidies with the primary objective of providing the public with satisfactory services at affordable fares. As discussed in chapter 2, while subsidies undoubtedly keep fares down, experience in the Third World is that they often lead to inefficiency and increasing costs. Rather than being satisfactory, services are inclined to deteriorate under these circumstances, particularly in the face of growing demand. Inevitably they require more and more subsidies, which often cannot be met by limited national or local government budgets. Authorities sometimes grant public transport subsidies in the expectation that car users will be induced to use public transport. In the case of metros, they hope that bus users as well as motorists will be induced to use metros, leading to reduced road congestion. Experience has shown that these benefits expected from subsidies are often disappointing and difficult to sustain.

Operating subsidies, designed to cover operating losses, usually have a particularly adverse effect on services. On the one hand they are inclined to reduce the incentive of recipients to keep down costs and to increase revenues in order to minimise losses. On the other hand, with rising costs and demand, operators relying on subsidies face a constant battle with authorities to obtain sufficient subsidy to cover increasing deficits. In addition there is considerable reluctance on the part of aid agencies to provide assistance to services that receive large operating subsidies. Certainly loss making corporations face considerable difficulties in raising bank loans. A typical example is the Karachi Transport Corporation (KTC), which has a very low level of productivity and requires an operating subsidy in the region of US$ 5 million per year (see box 2.1). During a period when there were a number of fare increases, the resulting improved financial situation was quickly nullified by corresponding increases in costs. As a result, despite the fare increases, the subsidies could not be reduced. Because of its heavy reliance on operating subsidies, the corporation is quite unable to attract funds for needed improvements and expansion. KTC is by no means the recipient of the largest subsidy. For example, higher annual subsidies are received by bus corporations in Calcutta (US$10 million: equivalent to 4 cents per passenger), Cairo (US$26 million: 3 cents per passenger), and Bangkok (US$30 million: 2 cents per passenger). In Sao Paulo, the public bus service receives a massive annual subsidy of US$90 million, and with an annual patronage of about 650 million passengers, this is equivalent to almost 14 cents per passenger.

The use of capital subsidies as a means of funding urban transport infrastructure, rolling stock and equipment is widespread throughout the Third World. It does not raise the same objections usually associated with operating subsidies, and may, in fact, stimulate funding from other sources. Capital subsidies are usually justified on the basis that they will permit the provision or improvement of systems with widespread economic and social benefits. Often these benefits stretch beyond the immediate users and it may be difficult to capture from all the beneficiaries their share of the costs. Most of the Brazilian busways, with widespread benefits, receive capital subsidies for this reason, as do a number of metros.

Not infrequently capital subsidies are applied to prestige projects for political reasons unsupported by proper appraisal. Often in these cases, more appropriate, albeit less impressive options, are rejected. For example, in Lima, a costly elevated metro is replacing, in part, the segregated busway which has a very good performance record and is very cost effective. Less prestigious alternatives were rejected by top politicians. However, because of the high cost and future financial burden, the completion of the metro is now in doubt and could be a political embarrassment.

Capital subsidies can play an important part in capital intensive systems in which the interests of the private sector are being sought. In particular, they encourage private money to be forthcoming to fund the element of the cost that could be recovered from users in the form of tolls and fares. Capital subsidies also reassure investors of the commitment of governments to the success of proposed projects. They may be in the form of capital grants, government equity, and land or other assets at below market value. One or more of these devices has played an important part in a number of project financing packages.

PRIVATE INVESTMENT IN BUSES

A very considerable amount of private funds is invested in the vast fleets of private buses, minibuses, paratransit vehicles and taxis. However, the individual investments are comparatively small and funded from a variety of formal and informal sources: - commercial banks, development banks, unions, various types of entrepreneurs, loan sharks, and family savings. The majority of private operators are very small enterprises with few assets and thus find it difficult to meet criteria for commercial bank loans. Sometimes unions, cooperatives or route associations, have fared a little better in obtaining commercial bank loans for vehicles. This is because commercial banks prefer to deal with corporate companies with fixed assets, but these are few and far between in private sector bus operations. Small operators also have difficulties in obtaining suppliers' credits for much the same reasons. A number of governments have attempted to overcome this problem by the provision of funds, including foreign exchange, specifically ear-marked for small transport enterprises. However, little of this funding seems to have trickled down to urban bus operators. A notable exception is in Brazil where very substantial government lending, channelled through the National Development Bank, is a major source of funding for private bus companies.

While there may be a lack of formal financing, both big and small time entrepreneurs proliferate in the bus business. Despite the difficulties, they seem able to gain access to funds for the purchase of buses. They may have little interest in running buses but gladly hire them out in return for a sizable share of the fare box revenue.

JOINT VENTURES

In a number of cities transit systems, in particular bus companies, are funded and owned partly by public authorities and partly by private enterprises. Usually such companies operate under a contract with a government ministry. The government's obligations are to approve timely fare increases in line with rising costs, and to provide a subsidy to cover concessionary fares and a share of capital costs. On its part, the company usually finances and supplies the rolling stock and other equipment and is required to operate a specified quantity of buses and to meet agreed performance targets.

Experience with joint venture bus companies indicates that while superior services may be provided, these are rarely affordable to the majority of users. As a result, there is a strong risk of heavy subsidies. Fairly typical is the SOTRA bus company in Abidjan, a joint venture between the Cote D'Ivoire Government and Renault Vehicle Industries. The company was founded in 1960 and has a capital base of US$ 12 million. The state owns 60 per cent of the shares and Renault owns 40 per cent. The company, with a fleet of nearly 1000 large buses and 200 smaller buses, has much spare capacity. While it has proved to be very effective in providing high standard services, it is also very costly and requires an operating subsidy of over US$16 million per year.

FUNDING OF CAPITAL INTENSIVE TRANSIT SYSTEMS

The funding of the more capital intensive transit systems, such as metros, LRT, and segregated busways, has in the past been the prerogative of the public sector. This has often been with the assistance of overseas governments prepared to support the purchase of equipment and rolling stock from their own manufacturers (Table 11.1).

In the expectation that metros would be financially viable, cities have financed their metros mainly with foreign loans, with only a small amount of local lending. But with results well below expectations, most metro authorities are currently heavily in debt. In many cases the principal debt is carried or guaranteed by central government and it is this type of loan, which generates little or no financial return or foreign exchange, that has contributed most strongly to the Third World debt crisis.

TABLE 11.1
The funding of selected transit systems

City	Source of funding
Cairo Metro	73% French Government soft loans, remainder bank loans with some Government equity.
Calcutta Metro	Central Government with 4% contribution from Japan.
Delhi Metro (proposed)	To be equally shared between Indian central and local governments.
Hong Kong MTR	Government equity, land development revenue and commercial bank loans.
Istanbul LRT	Loans from Sweden and Austria with central government guarantees, some local government funds.
Manila LRT	Turn key contract; loans from Belgium Government and foreign banks with about 30% government equity.
Mexico City Metro	Partly French Government soft loans, partly French banks on commercial terms.
Porto Alegre Metro	Mainly Federal Government with World Bank loan.
Pusan Metro	Foreign debt arranged by municipal government, but taken over by Central Government.
Rio de Janeiro Metro	Partly by state of Rio de Janeiro and partly by Federal Government.
Santiago Metro	60% French Government soft loans, remainder local grants.
Sao Paulo Metro	State of Sao Paulo with some national bank loans.
Seoul Metro	Lines 1&2 metropolitan government, Lines 3&4 partly by private enterprise; subway bonds levied on car buyers.
Singapore Metro	Central Government.
Tunis LRT	75% German and Austrian Government soft loans; remainder local funds.

Source: TRL Research Report 278

In recent years there has been a growing interest by governments in obtaining private financing for expensive urban transport systems. Some governments have sought to raise private capital to support public sector transit systems, against property or land development. One of the most successful ventures has been the development of air space above the stations and depots of the Hong Kong Mass Transit Railway. Taking advantage of the enhanced land values in the vicinity of the railway, the transit corporation has entered into joint ventures with property developers. The developments have been undertaken at the cost and risk of the corporations' joint venture partners, with the corporation taking a share of the profits, generally about 50 per cent. As a result both commercial and residential developments have been undertaken with proceeds of sale making a significant contribution of about 10 per cent of railway construction costs. In addition, recurring rental income from retained commercial facilities makes a contribution of about 5 per cent to the corporations' revenue. Similar arrangements have been undertaken in the case of the Seoul Metro and are being planned in respect of the rail mass transit for Bangkok. Busways and LRT also lend themselves to land development opportunities of this type.

Currently private investment through Build Operate and Transfer (BOT) concessions, is attracting particular interest. Basically, BOT provides for private enterprises (concessionaires) to design, construct, finance and operate a transit system usually for a period of between 15 and 25 years. At the end of the agreement period, the assets are transferred to the government. To stimulate interest in such projects and to reassure interested bidders of their commitment, Governments may bear a share of the costs, or may contribute other assets such as land. The concessionaires are expected to bear most of the risks of construction, including delays, and the commercial risks of operation. In return for providing the systems, the concessionaires are allowed to retain fare box and other income derived by the systems. They are often very interested in any development opportunities, such as building rights over and around stations, mentioned above. The terms suggested by interested BOT bidders reflect the likely viability and risks involved. In particular, BOT enterprises usually press to have full control of fare schedules and other tariffs, and for protection from "unfair" competition by other public transport. They also call for protection from foreign exchange and security risks, and other risks, such as delays, that are seen to be beyond their control. BOT concessionaires are usually consortia of bankers, engineers, construction companies, equipment and rolling stock suppliers, public transport operators and possibly others. Because of the many factors involved including legal, political, social, financial, economic, environmental, engineering and management, BOT negotiations and contract preparations sometimes are spread over several years. Delays can be due to many issues, such as the contribution and part to be played by government, including the guaranteeing of loans, and the terms for the provision of land. While a number of urban bridges, tunnels and expressways have been constructed as BOT projects, no transit systems have yet been completed using BOT, although several are currently in the pipeline. At advanced stages of development are the BOT schemes for metros in Ankara and Bangkok (Box 11.1).

INTERNATIONAL AND BILATERAL AID

In comparison with other sectors, urban transport has received only a modest amount of international aid. Nevertheless, in the case of World Bank lending, the largest source of international aid, this has amounted to over US$ 2000 million in the last twenty years. This amount was in support of projects costing in total US$ 5000 million. Most of this lending is for urban road construction, maintenance and improvements. Bus services, including vehicles, facilities and priority schemes accounted for 12 per cent. Rail systems received only 3 per cent (Table 11.2).

To be eligible for World Bank loans (IBRD loans), a nation must have a per capita GNP under US$ 4080. Loans have to be guaranteed by the borrowing country and paid back over 15 to 20 years including a grace period of up to 5 years. The interest rate varies, but in recent years has been within the range of 7 to 8 per cent. For the poorer countries, generally those with per capita GNP under US$580, an affiliate of the World Bank, the International Development Association (IDA) provides credits, which are in effect interest-free loans. They have to be paid back over 50 years and include a 10 year grace period. Before loans or credits are approved they are subject to detailed appraisal.

Third World public transport systems receive a considerable amount of bilateral aid. A notable

BANGKOK MASS TRANSIT FINANCING.   BOX 11.1

Proposals to construct a mass transit railway in Bangkok to solve the city's chronic transport problems have been under consideration for a long time but failed to obtain any funding. In recent years the Government has sought to overcome the problems of funding and implementation by inviting participation of overseas private interests in Build Operate and Transfer ventures (BOT). In 1986, the Expressway and Rapid Transit Authority (ETA) invited bids for what is known as the Skytrain. In 1990, the Ministry of Transport and Communications invited bids for a combined elevated road and railway system. This would mainly make use of the existing right of way of the State Railway of Thailand (SRT), and would serve areas and movements different from those of the Skytrain.

The Skytrain project comprises the funding, construction and operation of the first phase of an elevated mass transit railway. The system consists of two lines with a total length of 34km, making a partial loop around the centre of Bangkok. The total cost of this project is estimated at US$1.6 billion. The terms provide for the Thai Government to take at least 25 per cent of the total equity when the final costs are determined. The balance would be raised by the successful consortium.

The opportunities provided by The Skytrain proposals have attracted considerable interest, with the result that there has been stiff competition amongst several international consortia to take part. This interest has continued despite more than five years of protracted and expensive negotiations. Eventually one consortia, led by Lavalin International of Canada, has became close to being awarded the concession. Lavalin intends to raise finance partly from mixed credits, mainly from Canada, with a smaller credit from Japan. Recent delays have been caused by difficulties in obtaining the Thai Government's guarantee of loans, and the resolution of other issues.

The roadway-railway invitation received only one bid, from Hopewell Holdings, an international development company based in Hong Kong. The bid, which has been accepted, is for a more extensive scheme than the invitation. It consists of the construction of 60km of elevated rail mass transit, with express toll roadways built above the railway. The system will have two lines, north-south and east-west, crossing close to the city centre. It will also serve the airport. The alignment, being mainly within SRT right of way, avoids the high land acquisition costs and problems associated with the Skytrain. Furthermore, in addition to the operation of the rail mass transit and management of the toll roads, the concession, which is for 30 years, permits the development of over 80 hectares of under-utilised SRT land at 5 sites. The total cost, estimated at US$2.8 billion, would be funded by US$ 400 million of equity held by Hopewell with US$ 1 billion in foreign debt and US$ 1.4 billion in local debt. In addition to revenue from railway fares and road tolls, the project is expected to generate very substantial profits from land development, including in particular the development opportunities offered by under-utilised SRT land.

donor of urban transport aid is Japan with lending on a par with that of the World Bank. Most of its aid is for railway projects and arterial highways principally in Asia. To a much lesser extent several European countries also provide aid for Third World public transport systems. This is mainly directed towards technical assistance and training with some aid for the supply of buses and metro technology.

TABLE 11.2
World Bank urban transport project costs, 1972-1991

Distribution of project costs by components

Component	US$ (millions)	Per cent
Road construction	1255	27.5
Street improvement	1071	23.5
Road maintenance	530	11.6
Traffic management	445	9.7
Bus rehab. and acquisition	278	6.1
Bus facilities	151	3.3
Bus priority schemes	116	2.5
Rail systems	366	8.0
Technical assistance	229	5.0
Training	24	0.5
Other	106	2.3
TOTAL	4571	100.0

Source: World Bank 1991

12 INSTITUTIONAL STRUCTURE

Urban transport in the Third World functions within a wide variety of institutional structures. The differences arise because cultures, politics, economies and geographic features vary considerably from one country to the next. Nevertheless, most institutional structures share a lack of strength and coordination.

The strength of urban transport institutions has a very considerable bearing on the effectiveness of public transport. At the national level strong institutions play a vital role by:

- monitoring public opinion and demands for public transport,
- formulating policies and programmes that facilitate and encourage the provision of services,
- enacting laws for the effective regulation of traffic and transport,
- developing procedures for the appraisal of public transport projects,
- establishing mechanisms to stimulate the funding of public transport,
- monitoring and coordination of policy and programme implementation.

Similarly, at the local level, institutions can play a vital role by:

- identifying the needs of the public and monitoring their concerns,
- planning, design, appraisal and implementation of projects to support public transport,
- the enforcement of traffic and public transport regulations,
- implementing funding mechanisms for public transport,
- monitoring and coordinating local public transport services and projects.

Countries with strong and effective urban transport institutional structures, able to cope with rising transport problems, are the exception in the Third World. More usually institutions, which may have been adequate in the past now find it difficult to keep pace with the rapid growth in demand and complexity of city transport. Commonly, institutions tend to be on the one hand overstaffed, but on the other hand seriously lacking in skilled and experienced staff. Often they are not geared for making the best use of resources, and may find it difficult to reap the benefits of advancing technology. Also, urban transport comprises many elements that need to be carefully coordinated and integrated to achieve optimum efficiency in the movement of people and goods. However, it is not unusual to find agencies, which should be coordinated, working almost in isolation, or even in opposition.

The experience of aid agencies, including the World Bank, is that institutional weakness is the primary reason for poor project implementation or performance. This can involve substantial cost and time over-runs, poor quality workmanship and materials, and returns and benefits falling far short of expectations. As a result most aid agencies place considerable emphasis on institutional strengthening and policy reform.

The institutional structure of many Third World countries is characterised by the large number of agencies with responsibilities for urban transport. In some of the larger cities federal, state, metropolitan, and local government agencies all play a part in the urban transport system. For example, in Calcutta there are at least 18 different government agencies responsible for dealing with public transport, roads and traffic. Lagos has a similar number (See Box 12.1). Under these

---

NIGERIA: URBAN TRANSPORT INSTITUTIONAL STRUCTURE   BOX 12.1

The urban transport institutional structure in Nigeria comprises several agencies at the national, state and local levels. Since their responsibilities are similar and over-lapping, and their priorities sometimes at variance, it is difficult to formulate and implement effective urban transport planning. The situation is particularly serious in Lagos, where the massive and complex transport problems call for detailed and coordinated programmes.

The institutional structure at the national level comprises:

- Federal Urban Mass Transit Programme (FUMTP). Under the authority of a Sole Administrator, with a small professional team, it is charged with revitalizing urban transport programmes in all of the states, with federal funding.

- Federal Road Safety Commission (FRCS). Responsible for reducing the very high rate of accidents in Nigeria. It provides a highway patrol function along federal roads.

- Federal Ministry of Transport (FMT). Responsible for overall transport policy but influence in urban areas is limited to suburban railways and ferries.

- Highway Department of the Federal Ministry of Works and Housing. Responsible for the national trunk road network. Because of the department's limited resources, important national trunk roads in urban areas are sorely neglected.

- Nigeria Police Force: Traffic and Motor Vehicle Division. Responsible for the enforcement of traffic laws and road safety. There is some confusion of the respective roles of the Traffic Police and National Road Safety Commission's highway patrols.

State agencies, using Lagos as an example, comprise:

- Lagos State Ministry of Works and Transport (MWT). Responsible for all "B" class roads, including traffic management. In Lagos traffic signals are shared between the State and the Federal Government. MWT is also responsible for the running of the state bus corporations,

- The Central Licensing Authority (within MWT). Responsible for the licensing and regulation of the private sector bus services. It lacks experience in public transport and is unable to enforce regulations.

- Lagos State Parking Authority. In charge of public car parks, and along with the Traffic Police and Traffic Wardens has the powers to apprehend and fine parking offenders.

- Lagos State Transport Corporation. Operates public sector bus services in Lagos under the Lagos State MWT.

The municipal governments in Nigeria are supposed to bear wide responsibilities for urban transport. However, this role has mainly been relegated to minor urban roads and the provision of motor vehicle parks and bus lay-bys. Generally, municipal governments are very poorly funded. They are not well coordinated and have inconsistent policies. This is a particular problem in Lagos which has five municipal areas and results in considerable variations in the condition of minor roads and a disjointed road network.

circumstances coordination and communication are particularly important but often sorely lacking. In some cases, because of jealously guarded positions, there is conflict rather than cooperation in dealing with problems. In other cases responsibilities are poorly defined or confused, so that the need for action is either overlooked, or at the other extreme, duplicated. As a result accountability is undermined and performance suffers. Often when institutions are found to be well structured and to posses competent staff, they are unable to function effectively because of a serious lack of funding.

Of the many components of urban transport, public transport is probably the most demanding on city authorities, and brings out any weaknesses or strengths in the institutional structure. The effectiveness of public transport is particularly dependent on there being a sound institutional basis for the formulation and implementation of policy and planning.

PUBLIC TRANSPORT POLICY AND PLANNING

Since urban public transport policy and planning requires many factors to be considered at a high level, it is not surprising to find that several ministries need, or expect, to be involved. For example, in Zimbabwe urban transport planning involves the following ministries:

- Economics, Finance, Planning and Development,
- Trade and Commerce,
- Transport,
- Industry and Technology, and
- Local Government, Rural and Urban Development.

Ministers concerned with planning have a strong interest in seeing that it conforms with their own particular policies and interests. A divergence of views is almost inevitable, and in fact, is healthy if issues are to be properly aired. But this often develops into conflicts or deeply entrenched positions, which are very difficult to resolve. As a result decisions are often seriously delayed particularly if they have to be referred to the Cabinet. Some countries attempt to overcome these difficulties by establishing high level planning bodies, for example planning commissions. However, these also are inclined to be bogged down by vested interests particularly when land development opportunities may arise. There is also a tendency for policy on the allocation of funds and other resources to be based on influence or power, rather on the basis of economic or social benefits. Pressure from powerful railway lobbies, for example, has resulted in the diversion of very scarce resources to the construction of metros without proper evaluation.

Agencies charged with implementing policy and developing plans, while being responsible to one particular ministry, are often under pressure from others. Also agencies working together on a project sometimes receive conflicting directions from their respective ministries. Once again this calls for strong institutional leadership and a structure that recognises the need for close cooperation and coordination of agencies.

The need to establish strong institutional structures has been well recognised by Brazil which set up EBTU (Empresa Brasileira dos Transportes Urbanos) with a view to providing coordinated

BRAZIL: EMPRESA BRASILEIRA DOS TRANSPORTES URBANOS (EBTU)
BOX 12.2

In 1976 the Federal Government, through the Ministry of Transport, set up
EBTU. It was established to promote and coordinate the implementation of the
national policy on urban transport. The policy had four main objectives:

-        efficiency in energy consumption,

-        maximum use of existing infrastructure,

-        improvement of urban transport systems, and

-        the integration of land use with urban transport.

EBTU was the main channel through which urban transport development funds
were granted to Metropolitan Regions (MRs), Conurbations (CBs) and
municipalities. It has been the only organisation capable of making
recommendations for the allocation of resources, preparing and supervising
projects and training programmes. EBTU developed programmes to improve
urban corridors, with particular emphasis on bus services and road safety.
Emphasis also was placed on the training of local municipal units to implement
bus transport and traffic engineering measures.

In preparing and evaluating projects EBTU built up a wealth of knowledge and
skills. These were distributed to urban transport authorities throughout the
country, mainly through the demonstrative effect of projects.

Initially EBTU programmes were financed by road user charges, a federal energy
programme, the World Bank and overseas commercial banks. In subsequent
years, these sources were reduced to funding by the World Bank and commercial
banks. With a decline in funding EBTU lost valuable leverage in effecting
improvements.

A serious weakness of the institutional structure as a whole was the lack of
coordination between EBTU and other federal agencies. For example much new
housing was built but left empty, because no provision was made for transport
services and infrastructure. EBTU was, in fact, not given responsibility for
coordination, which was included in the responsibilities of a committee which met
only every 2 months.

In the mid-1980's EBTU became increasingly involved in the direct
implementation of projects and grew very substantially from a small team of
experts to a multi-disciplined and unwieldy staff of over 600. The overall
effectiveness in undertaking its original tasks became impaired. Also the trend to
become involved in implementation of projects created much duplication of effort
with other agencies. As a result of these and other difficulties, and despite
considerable initial successes, the Federal Government decided to disband EBTU
in 1990.

and comprehensive country-wide urban transport programmes. While very successful in many
ways the organisation has not been without its weaknesses and political difficulties, and
eventually was disbanded. (See Box 12.2)

Because of a general lack of planning and design skills, most Third World urban transport
institutions rely heavily on the use of expatriate consultants. In all but the very undeveloped
countries, local consultants also participate but usually in a subordinate role to overseas
consultants. In order to strengthen local skills, most consultants' contracts require them to make
use of and train local staff. At the end of the assignment, these counter-part staff are expected to
be able to continue or replicate the work of the consultants. This approach has achieved mixed

results depending much on the choice of counter-part staff and the support they receive from their parent agencies during and after the assignment. A very good example has been the development of traffic management bureaux in Pakistan with the help of consultants. These bureaux are now able to undertake complex traffic management schemes with little outside assistance. Generally however, progress towards greater use of local staff has been slow despite much technical assistance and training. There is still a very strong tendency, when faced with problems or difficult decisions, hastily to call in overseas consultants, rather than giving due consideration to the use of local staff.

INSTITUTIONAL ARRANGEMENTS FOR BUS SERVICES

The main issues regarding the institutional arrangements for bus services concern ownership, funding, and the regulation of fares and operations. Ownership and operations have been reviewed in chapter 2, fares in Chapter 10 and funding in Chapter 11. The institutional arrangements for the regulation of bus operations are generally divided between institutions for the licensing and routing of buses, and those for the inspection of vehicles and drivers. These institutions generally only control private sector operators. Public corporations follow standards determined either by their boards or their parent ministries. In India extensive monitoring and coordination of standards of the State Road Transport Undertakings is effectively undertaken by the Central Institute of Road Transport, Pune. More than 60 undertakings with a combined fleet of over 100,000 buses are involved.

The Licensing of Buses. This is usually the responsibility of regional or city transport authorities. Their powers may permit them to specify the types of vehicles that can be used for bus services and the routes upon which they may operate. Through these powers they are also able to control the numbers and types of buses available in the city as a whole and, in some cities, each bus route. As discussed in Chapter 2, these powers may be exercised with the advice or veto of the traffic police, the traffic engineers, public bus corporations and/or the bus operators unions. The net result of excessive licensing conditions is that either the necessary expansion of services is severely inhibited or, under pressure of market forces, the regulations are blatantly disregarded.

Inspection of Buses and Drivers. In some cities these tasks are included in the responsibilities of the licensing authority, in others they are undertaken by the police. While most countries require all buses to be regularly inspected, and drivers to be tested, few vehicle testing stations are adequately staffed or equipped for this purpose. Generally the number of vehicles that should be inspected is so great in relation to the number of inspectors that, at the best, only the nominal inspection of a selection of vehicles is undertaken; at the worst, the stations serve only as a means of collecting inspection fees and bribes. A similar situation exists with regard to driver testing. Exceptionally, effective vehicle and driver testing is found in a number of Third World countries working within sound institutional frameworks. For example, both South Korea and Mexico have strict vehicle inspection procedures as part of their programmes to reduce air pollution.

BUSWAY TRANSIT

The institutional structure for the ownership, operation and regulation of busways can involve most of the agencies concerned with public transport plus several more. The main agencies directly involved may be at either federal, regional or municipal level and usually comprise the:

-    highway authority for the roads along which the busway is located,

-    public works department responsible for construction and maintenance of the busway infrastructure,

-    transport authority for the management of the busway and the regulation of buses using the busway,

-    traffic police for the enforcement of traffic regulations, in particular the unauthorised use of the busway, and

-    bus operators: in some cities, for example Abidjan, a single operator has exclusive use of the busways, in others such as Sao Paulo, services are operated by a municipal company and by numerous private companies.

Some of these functions may be combined into a single agency. For example, in Sao Paulo the municipal bus company takes on the responsibility for managing the system, security of passengers and dealing with breakdowns. Ownership may be held by federal ministries or municipal governments, or by bodies set up specifically for the purpose. Because of institutional complexities, busways seldom, if ever, are in the hands of private ownership. This may change with the interest being shown in the BOT financing of busways, as proposed, for example in Karachi.

URBAN RAIL SYSTEMS

Almost all suburban railways are owned and operated as part of national rail systems, and are thus within the public sector. They normally answer directly to federal governments which often makes integration with other parts of the urban transport system difficult. National railways fiercely defend their urban lines and are usually powerful in pressing for rail options as a solution to urban transport deficiencies.

Most tram and LRT systems are publicly owned and operated by municipal corporations. One notable exception is the Manila LRT. While this system is owned by the Light Rail Transit Authority, (a government corporation), operation and maintenance is in the hands of a private sector company, Metro Inc. under a ten year contract. (See Box 7.2)

In the case of metros, which are almost entirely within the public sector, it is usual to make a distinction between ownership and management. Ownership is generally in the hands of government at either national, regional or metropolitan level. For management and operation public corporations have been set up. Generally these have some degree of autonomy, and are relatively free of outmoded civil service attitudes to work practices and management procedures. However none is completely independent because of its heavy reliance on government capital and sometimes operating subsidies.

13 ENVIRONMENTAL IMPACT OF URBAN TRANSPORT

By far the greatest and most widespread effect of urban transport on the environment is due to air pollution and energy consumption by road vehicles. Other impacts, such as noise, water pollution, visual intrusion, social disruption and ecological damage, are generally less extensive but often have very serious local impacts, and may be of particular concern in suburban areas.

AIR POLLUTION

Because of the much lower levels of motorisation, the Third World accounts for only about 20 per cent of global transport energy consumption: the United States alone accounts for nearly 35 per cent. Studies undertaken by the World Bank estimate that transport in the Third World accounts for only 4 per cent of global emissions of fossil carbon dioxide, as compared to 18 per cent due to the industrialized countries. No more than 30 per cent of toxic motor vehicle emissions, such as carbon monoxide (CO), hydrocarbons (HC) and oxides of nitrogen (NOx) can be attributed to the Third World. The contribution to total lead and diesel particulates may be slightly higher than 30 per cent because of the poor quality of fuels and greater use of diesel vehicles in the Third World.

While the overall global effect of Third World transport currently is comparatively small, levels of automotive pollution in many large Third World cities is appalling, and a source of very considerable concern. This state of affairs is due to a number of reasons. For example, in Bangkok chronic air pollution is attributed to a rapidly growing and badly maintained vehicle fleet. Also, diesel fuel is of a poor quality and at a low price which encourages excessive use. In several cities in India, air pollutants greatly exceed internationally accepted levels, due mainly to the rapid growth and ageing of small vehicles such as motor cycles and auto-rickshaws, and the high lead content in gasoline. In Jakarta, severe traffic congestion coupled with extensive use of badly maintained two-stroke motor cycles and diesel trucks and buses results in very high and extensive air pollution. Because of the very crowded conditions and life styles in these cities, a very high proportion of the inhabitants are affected by air pollution and continuously exposed to considerable health hazards. Altitude, topography and climatic conditions may add very seriously to levels and the effects of air pollution, as in the case of Mexico City, the largest and one of the most motorized and heavily polluted cities in the world. (See Box 13.1)

With rapid growth in both urbanization and motorisation, the global effect and city level of automotive air pollution in the Third World is increasing significantly. Not only are conditions deteriorating in the many large cities already in trouble, but also in smaller cities which at present are not seriously affected. However, some of these, such as the secondary cities in Africa, may be spared the serious problems of air pollution for some time.

MEXICO CITY: AUTOMOTIVE AIR POLLUTION   BOX 13.1

The combination of 20 million people, 4 million motor vehicles, abundant sunshine, an altitude of 7400 feet, and being located in a basin surrounded by mountains, creates for Mexico City some of the most difficult environmental situations found anywhere in the world. Automotive air pollution, in particular, is a major concern.

The 4 million motor vehicles are mainly private cars but include 300,000 trucks, and very active fleets of minibuses and taxis (120,000) and buses (13,000). Many of these vehicles are more than 10 years old and few are fitted with effective anti-pollution devices. Together they emit some 4 million tons of pollutants into the atmosphere each year. An additional 1 million tons is attributed to industrial and other sources.

Because of the climatic and topographical conditions, much of this pollution is trapped at street level. Conditions in the winter, when inversion occurs, are particularly severe. The situation is aggravated by the high altitude which reduces engine efficiency and increases the emission of pollutants, and by the sunshine which stimulates photochemical smog.

The high levels of CO, HC, NOx, diesel particulates and lead found in Mexico City constitute a very serious health hazard for a large proportion of the inhabitants. The levels are many times those considered safe by the World Health Organisation (WHO). For example, in 1988 the CO level frequently exceeded 47 parts per million (ppm) compared to the WHO guide line of 9 ppm and the ozone level was consistently 60 times higher than the WHO safe level. Almost 70 per cent of new born babies in Mexico City show excessive levels of lead in their blood.

Because of its deep concern about this unsatisfactory situation the Government has been vigorously pursuing a package of measures to counter air pollution in Mexico City. In recent years it has progressively improved emission standards for gasoline-powered vehicles with permitted levels reduced by roughly 50 per cent since 1989. For automobiles, standards currently stand at CO: 11.2 g/mile, HC: 1.12 g/mile, and NOx 2.24 g/mile. They are scheduled to be further reduced to 3.40, 0.40 and 1.00 g/mile respectively by 1994, in line with current US EPA (1983) standards. Similar reductions have been made for gasoline engined commercial vehicles, with levels scheduled to be CO: 14, HC: 1.00 and NOx: 1.00 g/mile by 1994. Since 1990 all new private cars have had to be fitted with catalytic converters and regulations are being introduced to require new and existing minibuses also to be fitted with catalytic converters. This in turn will require greater use of unleaded fuels. In the case of emission standards for diesel engined vehicles, particularly new buses, the trend is towards strict USA (California) standards. All vehicles are subject to random and bi-annual inspections to check compliance with emission and other standards. The Government also has a policy of encouraging greater use of public transport and discouraging use of private cars. With a system of restricting the use of private cars by requiring motorists to leave their cars at home one working day each week, gasoline consumption has been reduced by more than 12 per cent with an appreciable reduction in air pollution.

Counter-measures undertaken in developing countries specifically to reduce air pollution mainly focus on various means of controlling vehicle emissions, and use of improved fuels. Other measures, such as the use of alternative fuels, traffic engineering, greater use of public transport and land use planning, often taken primarily for other reasons, also help reduce air pollution.

VEHICLE EMISSION CONTROLS

While many Third World countries have introduced legislation to control vehicle emissions, few follow this up with effective enforcement. Where emission limits for vehicles have been introduced, the required regular inspections, if undertaken at all, often are slip-shod and ineffective. In some places attendance at inspection centres is purely a formality and provides the opportunity for little more than the collection of inspection fees and "commissions". Other countries are inhibited from taking effective action to control emissions because of the level of technology and the costs involved.

The countries most susceptible to air pollution are, more often than not, also those with levels of technology and earnings sufficiently high to be able to introduce effective counter-measures. Nevertheless, the extent to which action is being taken varies considerably from country to country. Examples of countries pursuing vehicle emission controls, but with varying degrees of commitment, include Brazil, which has established strict vehicle emission limits and generally has applied World Health Organisation (WHO) and 1981 U.S Environmental Protection Agency (EPA) pollution standards. As from Jan 1992, the emission limits for most alcohol and gasoline-engined vehicles have been CO: 12g/km; HC: 1.2g/km and NOx 1.4g/km. Mexico similarly has set strong air pollution limits (See Box 13.1) as has South Korea with a very active air pollution control programme including random roadside inspections as well as regular inspections. Taiwan, which also carries out random roadside inspections, provides free motor cycle and bus emission and maintenance checks. The European emission standards adopted by Taiwan for new vehicles in 1987 are being replaced by the more stringent 1983 US EPA standards. Both Hong Kong and Singapore have adopted strict emission standards and carry out random and routine tests of all vehicles. Vehicles not meeting the required standards attract heavy fines, and may be impounded. India has developed its own standards based on the EEC requirements but modified to meet local conditions. Idle CO emissions may not exceed 3 per cent by volume for gasoline motor vehicles, or 4.5 per cent for motor cycles and auto-rickshaws. Maximum diesel smoke density limits have also been set at 75 HSU at full load.

USE OF UNLEADED AND ALTERNATIVE FUELS

Fuels used in many countries in the Third World are of a poor environmental quality, and may have excessive lead in the case of gasoline and excessive sulphur in the case of diesel fuel. In line with industrial countries, some of the more advanced developing countries, such as South Korea, Taiwan, Turkey, Chile, and Malaysia, have taken steps to reduce lead content in fuels and also to make greater use of unleaded gasoline. For example, Taiwan, as well as introducing unleaded gasoline, has also reduced the lead content of regular gasoline to below 0.12 gm/litre. But little use of unleaded fuel is made in the remainder of the Third World where lead content of regular gasoline is often as high as 0.8 gm/litre.

Alternatives to gasoline and diesel fuel have been used in a number of countries, mainly in expectation of economic as well as environmental benefits. For example, for many years Brazil has widely used alcohol from sugar to fuel motor vehicles (See Box 13.2). The benefits are that alcohol does not need lead and emits less CO, HC and NOx than gasoline. However, with the use

In the 1970's a depressed world market for sugar corresponded with the spiralling cost and shortages of oil. Making the best of the situation, in 1975 the Brazilian Government embarked on a very innovative programme to produce alcohol fuel from sugar. The product, ethanol, is used on its own or mixed with gasoline to produce what is called gasohol. The programme has been very successful technically, with an estimated 33 per cent of all passenger vehicles using ethanol and 65 per cent gasohol. The balance of 2 per cent run on diesel fuel. As a result dependence on imported oil has been significantly reduced. However, the programme has involved massive government subsidies with economic losses from inception in 1975 to 1988 estimated by the World Bank to be $1.8 billion.

The programme has several environmental advantages over the use of gasoline. Firstly, ethanol is far less susceptible to evaporation than gasoline and, as a result in the hot climate experienced in Brazil, far less pollutants evaporate into the air. Second, emissions of CO, HC, NOx and unburnt fuel are substantially less. Third, alcohol has a high octane rating and does not require the addition of lead. However, as well as its high cost, use of ethanol has the disadvantage that it produces dangerous emissions such as acetaldehyde which is linked to respiratory problems and is suspected of causing cancer. Also the process of making ethanol creates very large amounts of waste products, some hazardous, which create considerable disposal problems.

While gasohol can be used in gasoline engines, avoiding costly conversion, the high content of gasoline, usually about 80 - 90 per cent, wipes out most of the environmental advantages of using ethanol alone. Also, since the introduction of the scheme, the cost of sugar has risen on international markets, reducing the commercial interest in producing ethanol. The resulting shortage, due also to recent poor crops of sugar, has forced the government to import ethanol at considerable expense.

of alcohol more amounts of various aldehydes are burnt off. These include acetaldehyde, which is linked to respiratory problems and is suspected of causing cancer.

Only limited use by motor vehicles is made of other alternatives to gasoline such as liquified petroleum gas (LPG) and compressed natural gas (CNG). Examples of comparatively large users are Korea and Thailand with large fleets of taxis run on LPG. While LPG and CNG may be less polluting and more efficient than gasoline and diesel, having to be stored under pressure, and various other technical and distribution difficulties, currently reduce their attractiveness to most developing countries.

Many countries have considered the greater use of electrically powered public transport as a means of saving fossil fuels and reducing air pollution. However, the results have usually been disappointing, with high costs greatly out-weighing any savings. A study in Brazil of fossil fuel saving found that an investment of $1.5 billion in electric powered mass transport would result in an annual saving equivalent to only 1.2 days consumption of fossil fuels by the country as a whole. The use of electric cars is receiving considerable attention but has yet to emerge as a viable means of transport. Any local benefits need to be weighed against pollution at the source of power generation, and it is far from certain that the net gain, if any, would justify the likely higher vehicle and operation costs. The use of trolleybuses is reviewed in Chapter 3.

TRAFFIC MANAGEMENT AND OTHER COUNTER MEASURES

Over the years traffic management has received growing acceptance by Third World transport authorities as a means of reducing road congestion and traffic accidents and increasing the efficiency of public transport. In recent years its substantial environmental benefits have also been acknowledged. The primary justification for traffic management schemes has generally been on the basis of the economic benefits of reduced journey times and vehicle operating costs, in particular reduced fuel consumption. However, it is clear that improved traffic flow and reduction of fuel consumption also substantially reduce harmful vehicle emissions: most damaging to the environment is the creation of air pollution by the stop-start progress of vehicles in traffic jams. For example the traffic flow improvement measures in the First Mexico Urban Transport Project, funded by the World Bank, are estimated to reduce CO, HC and NOx emissions by approximately 25 per cent along the routes improved.

Many countries in the Third World are increasingly pursuing policies to encourage greater use of public transport and to restrain the use of private cars. The primary intention is to make more economic use of limited road space and other resources, but clearly these measures also reduce energy consumption and vehicle emissions. It has been estimated that private cars in Rio de Janeiro,require 12500kcal per passenger while urban buses use no more than 1800kcal per passenger. Pollution by buses individually may leave much to be desired, but their greater use in place of cars represents more economic use of fuel and very significant reduction in total emissions. In their use of energy, buses also compare favourably with other urban modes of transport, including rail systems (Figure 13.1).

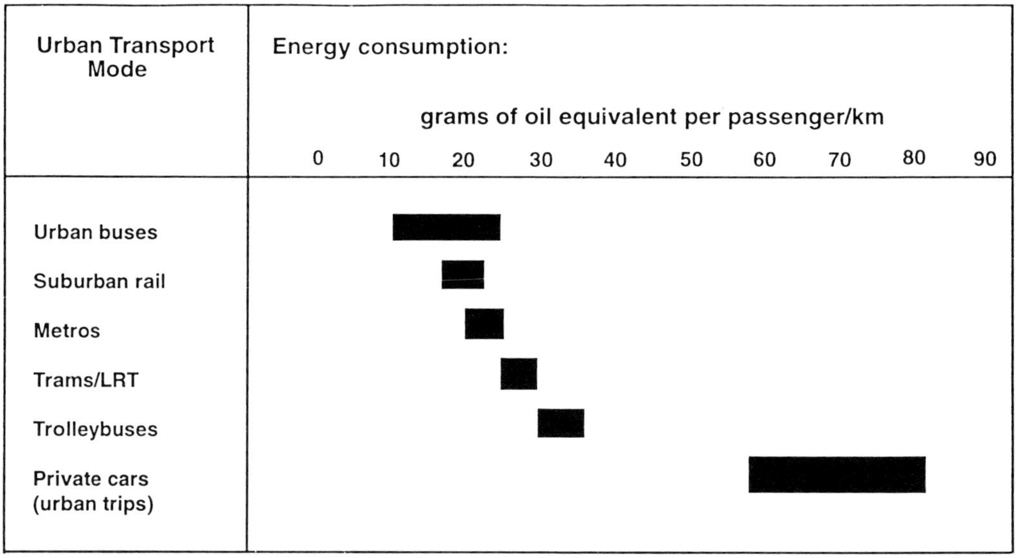

Source: Beauvais and Pillet, 1981

Fig 13.1   Energy Efficiency of Urban Transport Modes

94

Land use planning provides significant opportunities to reduce journey distances and travel times. As with traffic management, it can reduce fuel consumption and hence air pollution. While a number of Third World countries undertake land use planning few are able to implement it effectively. In particular they are inhibited by the effects of vested interests, corruption, unreliable land ownership records and uncontrollable squatting.

OTHER ENVIRONMENTAL IMPACTS

In only a few Third World cities is any appreciable concern shown for noise, water pollution, visual intrusion, social disruption and ecological damage that may arise because of urban transport. Often legal limits are imposed on noise and in some places statutory vehicle inspections include testing noise levels, but enforcement is usually lax. Buses parked at terminals with their engines running are a frequent source of complaints, particularly in the early morning. Water pollution due to the discharge of waste vehicle oil is very serious in some cities but counter-measures are rare. For example, in Lagos very high concentrations of oil in Lagos Lagoon are attributed to the dumping of sump oil into the drainage system, but little is done to stop this practice.

In the past there may have been a general lack of consideration for the environment, but in recent years there has been growing recognition of the need to reduce the environmental impact of transport in cities. As an encouraging step in this direction, in some cities environmental impacts are considered when large projects are planned and evaluated. In particular, environmental impact studies are now an important part of the appraisal of projects to be financed by aid agencies such as the World Bank and the Overseas Development Adminstration. In these cases the projects include the counter measures needed to avoid or minimise environmental impacts. This commendable approach by aid agencies has improved project implementation, and while it may have little direct impact beyond project boundaries, it has proved to be valuable in creating a greater local awareness of environmental problems caused by urban transport.

A number of countries are beginning to consider the much broader opportunities for protecting the environment of their cities. For example, Bangkok with its very serious environmental problems has embarked on a comprehensive environmental action plan for transport. This covers:

-       air pollution control,
-       noise abatement,
-       land development to avoid urban sprawl and to reduce journeys,
-       policy to influence traffic levels and mix of public transport modes,
-       segregation of sensitive land uses from heavy traffic flows,
-       reducing severance created by major infrastructure, and
-       environmental management to minimise the impact of public and private projects.

14 URBAN PUBLIC TRANSPORT: THE FUTURE

With very considerable differences between countries in the Third World, it is inevitable that they will face a very mixed future. The present extremes of economic growth and decline, and of order and chaos, can be expected to continue, and may widen. In the case of urban transport, the future situation in each country, or for that matter in each city, will depend on a large number of factors. Of particular influence are likely to be economic development, the growth in demand, government policies including institutional strengthening, appropriate aid and available technology.

ECONOMIC DEVELOPMENT

The current trend of slow, and in some cases declining, economic growth, can be expected to continue. While the prospects may be good, at least in the short run, for a few countries such as Indonesia, Malaysia, and Thailand, for many others the forecasts are for little more than zero growth or even negative growth in per capita terms. The hardest hit are likely to be non-oil producing countries, and those torn by war or civil strife. Of particular concern is the future economic development of sub-Saharan Africa where the decline in GDP per capita is currently greater than 2.0 per cent per annum.

Countries with improving economies will have to contend with growing demand for the ownership and use of private cars with the prospects of worsening traffic congestion. However, these countries will be better able to afford road improvements, traffic management and the use of improved public transport. The direction in which they progress will depend on Government policy.

In the case of countries at the other extreme, negative economic growth with declining real incomes will have a very damaging impact on urban transport. In the first place, fierce competition for scarce government funds can be expected. Under these circumstances cuts in allocations for road improvements and maintenance, subsidies for public transport and traffic management are inevitable. For the users, declining real incomes will reduce their ability to afford public transport. In turn, with falling revenues, services will shrink and deteriorate as is currently the situation in several countries in Africa. For example, bus fleets in Sierra Leone, Sudan and Uganda were cut by more than half between 1980 and 1990 and are continuing to decline.

Conditions in the majority of countries, although less extreme, are forecast to show only little or very moderate growth in the short term. Many may require aid and policy reforms in order to make any appreciable headway in coping with their urban transport problems. Certainly the amount of growth and level of earnings will provide only slender opportunities for the upgrading of transport systems so sorely needed in most Third World countries.

GROWTH IN DEMAND

Rapid growth in demand for urban transport services and road capacity is likely to be a continuing feature in most Third World cities. The main factors prompting this growth are the increases in urban population and in motorisation.

United Nations population forecasts indicate that the unprecedented growth in urban populations of the 1980's will continue in the 1990's. Between 1990 and 2000 urban populations are expected to increase in Africa by 4.7 per cent per annum; in Asia by 3.0 per cent and in Latin America by 2.6 per cent. As a result, this decade will see the population of most cities in Africa increase by about 50 per cent. Some, such as Lagos, Lusaka, Dar Es Salaam, Blantyre, and Nairobi, will double or nearly double in size. In absolute terms the largest increases are expected to take place in Asia with the urban population of India increasing by 600,000 each month. Calcutta and Bombay are forecast to top 16 million, and Delhi 13 million by 2000. The urban population of China is expected to grow by 3.0 per cent each year and to reach 300 million by 2000. With more than 70 per cent of the population of Latin America already living in cities and towns, the rate of urban growth is expected to somewhat slacken. However, the region will be home to the largest cities in the world, with the population topping 26 million in Mexico City and 24 million in Sao Paulo by 2000.

As a result of these urban population increases the future demand for urban transport in the Third World will be staggering. In terms of buses alone, even with increased use of rail, it has been estimated that the current bus fleet of roughly 1.2 million will need to be increased to at least 2.2 million by year 2000 in order to be brought up to strength.

Global figures for motor vehicles are estimated to show only modest increases of 2-3 per cent per annum in the coming years, with the past dramatic increases experienced in some developing countries being reversed. For example, in Nigeria, very sharp increases in the early 1980's were followed in 1988 by several years with decreases of about 20 per cent per annum. In many other African countries, motorisation is expected to show little if any increase, and may decline, at least in the short term. Where the rate of car ownership is reducing, traffic flow may be improved but the heavy burden on hard pressed public transport will increase. In contrast, above average increases in private car and motorcycle use can be expected in countries, mainly in Asia, with moderate economic growth. Such increases will add to congestion, undermine public transport and create considerable pressure to invest in more road capacity, a process which many countries can ill afford.

GOVERNMENT POLICIES

The extent to which countries will be able to cope with future demand and make the best use of resources will be greatly influenced by the policies they adopt. Pressure to follow sound policies will arise, not only from public discontent with poor travelling conditions, but also from aid agencies seeking to strengthen development and safeguard the aid they provide. The political will to implement effective polices, particularly those which may be unpopular (eg restraints on car use), will be a major factor in determining which cities will be able to provide adequate urban transport systems and those that will fall behind.

Past experience worldwide has shown that the policies most likely to lead to more satisfactory urban transport in the future provide for:

- restraints in the use of private cars coupled with improved public transport,
- comprehensive traffic management, road improvements and maintenance with emphasis on benefits to public transport,
- measures to encourage greater participation of the private sector in the provision of urban transport services, with the minimum of regulation,
- effective regulation and inspection of vehicles to promote safety and protect the environment,
- measures to minimise the opportunities for corruption, particularly with regard to the enforcement of traffic and transport regulations, including vehicle and driver testing,
- the funding and selection of projects on the basis of sound financial, economic and environmental appraisals,
- strengthening and adequate funding of urban transport institutions, including the strengthening of financial services for urban transport development.

Many countries with a desire to overcome severe urban transport problems, and to minimise public spending, already pursue these policies to varying extents. Even those countries that traditionally rely heavily on the public sector and extensive regulation are increasingly turning towards more liberal policies. Because of the favourable experience with these policies throughout the world, and in the face of growing demands and meagre resources, more and more cities can be expected to follow suit in the future.

INTERNATIONAL AND BILATERAL AID

Since many countries will continue to find it difficult to mobilise enough resources to meet the future transport needs of their cities, there will continue to be very considerable demand for outside assistance. However, international aid is having to be spread wider with the breakdown of central economies in Eastern and Central Europe and the continuing very heavy demands of other sectors, such as agriculture and energy. As a result, urban transport in the Third World is likely to face very stiff competition for international aid. World Bank lending for urban transport is expected to continue at its current level of roughly US$100 million per annum, with greater emphasis on projects promising high economic returns and favourable city wide impacts on productivity, poverty and the environment.

Many foreign governments providing bilateral aid for Third World urban transport can be expected to continue with their programmes, but these also may be effected by calls for urgent aid for Eastern Europe and the former Soviet Union. One of the largest donors, the Japanese Government is expected to continue to play a dominant role in the Third World, particularly in Asia. Its lending for urban transport is likely to continue to average about US$80 million per annum. While it favours major highway and railway projects, rather than low cost solutions, its future policy, like that of the World Bank, will emphasise the importance of institutional development in order to build up local planning, implementation and operational capabilities. Bilateral aid from some foreign governments is expected to continue to be more related to the needs of their own industries to export surplus capacity, rather than the needs of the recipient countries.

TECHNOLOGY

Urban transport technology is growing rapidly in the industrial countries both in terms of variety and sophistication. Much of this may transfer well to Third World countries, depending on the level of technical experience and skills required. However, some technology being pressed on developing countries is well beyond local skills and experience. Certainly for the Third World to be able to take full advantage of new technology there is a considerable need to provide for appropriate development of local skills. Clearly, if the mammoth urban transport problems in developing cities are to be solved, then every opportunity for appropriate technology advancement needs to be pursued in all the components of urban transport (Plate 14.1).

Demand Management. Many cities in the future will have little option but to restrain the use of private cars despite this being unpopular with motorists. Demand management itself is a comparatively new technology, with area licensing having been pioneered by Singapore in 1975 (Box 9.3). The future opportunities for electronic road pricing are quite considerable, and technically are not beyond the bounds of some of the more advanced developing countries. The choice of system will need to take into account problems which abound in some countries, such as theft or damage of equipment, revenue collection, enforcement, corruption, and identification of drivers, in particular defaulters.

Traffic Management. Greater use of low cost, high return solutions such as traffic management, can be expected in the future. The more advanced countries are likely to take advantage of the various sophisticated area traffic control and surveillance systems available. However, many countries first need to master the operation and maintenance of comparatively simple traffic signals before attempting to up-grade.

Land Use Management. With mounting urban problems city authorities are likely to come under increasing pressure to put more effort into land use management. While this may have not been very effective in the past, any trend towards careful design and enforcement of land use plans could substantially reduce the demand for public transport services. In particular, work trips, which constitute the bulk of urban travel, would be reduced by zoning employment opportunities away from city centres and close to residential areas.

Telecommunications. The greater emphasis being given to the improvement of telecommunication systems can be expected to provide considerable benefits to urban transport. Firstly, inadequate and unreliable telephone systems result in very many otherwise avoidable journeys having to be undertaken to hold discussions and to pass messages. In some cities these journeys add very considerably to traffic flow and congestion. Secondly, poor telephone systems tend to inhibit balanced land use, as in the case of Caracas, where bad congestion is partly due to the concentration of offices in the city centre because of the wide practice of passing messages by couriers rather than by telephone. Studies in India indicate that industries are reluctant to move to development areas designed to minimise transport needs because telecommunications are not reliable. Thirdly, many high technology transport systems, such as area traffic control and

Plate 14.1a   Developments in technology: pneumatically driver Aeromovel, Porto Alegre, Brazil

Plate 14.1b   Developments in bus organisation: raised bus stands for faster boarding and alighting of bus passengers, Curitiba, Brazil

Plate 14.1c   Modern bus interchange facilities, Mexico City

surveillance, make use of telecommunication networks for relaying data and commands between terminals and control centres. One of the arguments for the improvement of the telephone system in Karachi is based on the future comprehensive area traffic control systems planned for the city. The growing use of telefax and computer links generally will also somewhat tend to reduce traffic flow in the future.

BUS SERVICES

Because of growing demand for bus services coupled with greater concern for the environment in the future, there is likely to be pressure for higher capacity bus systems and buses with improved safety and environmental characteristics. Increased capacity will doubtless be met by more extensive provision of priority for buses in the form of exclusive bus lanes and busways. There may also be a tendency towards larger buses provided this is not inhibited by policy and regulation. Nevertheless, a greater emphasis in the future on market forces is likely to see much more variety in the size and quality of buses and competition between operators.

The technology of bus priority systems is advancing and the future is likely to see more elevated busways being constructed. In some cases the designs may permit conversion to LRT or rapid rail when justified by demand and economic returns. For example, Karachi authorities plan to have in place a 85km transitway (bus/LRT) network, mainly elevated, by 2001. For busways to be successful, appropriate institutional and financial arrangements with good cooperation between the public and private sectors will be needed.

Various traffic signal systems have been developed, particularly in the United Kingdom, to provide priority to buses. Some of these systems, tried only in a very limited way in developing countries, may be introduced more widely in the future. The more simple of these are computerised area traffic control systems designed to favour traffic streams containing buses. Other, more sophisticated systems, using transponders on buses, are able to detect approaching buses and activate traffic signals in their favour. All these systems depend on skilled designers and controllers, and high technical standards of operation and maintenance. They also depend heavily on other road users obeying traffic signals and thus require higher standards of enforcement than currently found in most developing cities.

Inevitable pressure in the future to improve safety and environmental quality is likely to lead to the introduction of standards based on USA or European requirements. However, success will greatly depend on the political will to see that the standards are effectively enforced. Without considerable outside assistance, little improvement can be expected in low income countries. Without help, many of these will continue to have little option but to make use of old and dilapidated buses and minibuses, and are unlikely to give much priority to safety and environmental considerations.

RAIL SERVICES

There is considerable Third World interest in railway investment as a means of meeting urban travel demands. The future opportunities for appropriate investment in rail are likely to arise mainly in cities with existing railways ripe for upgrading to commuter standards. For some years to come, there can only be limited prospects for new metro systems in the Third World despite their obvious attractiveness. Because of the very high costs of metros, only in cities with high levels of earnings can they be expected to achieve acceptable economic returns. As far as financial viability is concerned, there can be little chance of improvement even in the long term. On the basis of experience in industrialised countries, most cities will be quite unable to afford to build and run metros without massive financial and technical assistance. This is unlikely to be forthcoming from international aid agencies because they are inclined to favour more cost effective solutions. Most assistance is apt to be in the form of bilateral aid and suppliers credits but this is most unlikely to cover future operational losses and depreciation. Private investment in metros (eg BOT) may only be forthcoming with substantial government guarantees, land concessions and subsidies.

Despite the financial consequences of building and running metros, cities with existing systems continue to plan new lines and extensions. TRL studies have found this to be true in respect of every one of 15 cities with metros that were studied. For example, in Sao Paulo there are plans to extend the existing 28km metro to 78 km in the next four years, despite crippling subsidies. However, in a number of cases, for example Mexico City and Calcutta, extensions are planned to be LRT in order to cut costs substantially. In others plans have been shelved, at least for the time being, because of costs.

Compared with full metros, the future of LRT in the Third World is comparatively bright, since it is likely to be much more affordable. As economies and incomes rise, more countries should be able to justify LRT in terms of comfort, safety and speed. However it is difficult to justify LRT on the basis of capacity: recent studies indicate that busways can match, and in some circumstances exceed, the capacity of LRT. Busways are also far more cost effective and compatible with local technology and skills. Nevertheless, the growing world wide interest in LRT is likely to promote technical advances in the future which improve its cost effectiveness and feasibility for developing countries.

CONCLUSION

While there are very considerable differences between cities in the Third World, almost all share a common future of continuing rapid growth in population leading to a corresponding growth in demand for public transport. With severe resource constraints, most cities will face a constant battle to meet that demand. Nevertheless, the way in which some cities have tackled their public transport problems provides a measure of optimism that solutions can be found.

This state of the art review embraces many cities and has drawn on data and research from a very wide number of sources. The range of information provided should assist decision makers to consider options appropriate for dealing with the particular problems of their own cities. It should also provide a lead for studies and more in-depth research to formulate detailed solutions, including choice of technology, funding, energy conservation and environmental protection.

Clearly Third World cities provide considerable scope for research, for the development of innovative technology, and for provision of worthwhile aid - a challenge that many concerned with public transport will find difficult to resist.

BIBLIOGRAPHY

Note: This review of public transport is based on very extensive material and observations covering some sixty-five cities in the Third World. For practical purposes the bibliography is confined to general reference material and selected publications and papers of broad interest.

GENERAL REFERENCES (applicable to several chapters)

Asian Development Bank, 1989. *Review of the scope for Bank assistance to urban transport.* Infrastructure Department, Asian Development Bank, Manila.

Bushell C. and P.Stonham (editors), 1991. *Jane's urban transport systems.* Jane's Information Group, London.

Economic Commission for Africa, 1991. Urban transport: a baseline assessment and stategy for the Second United Nations Transport and Communications Decade for Africa. ECA, Addis Ababa.

Heraty M.J.(editor-in-chief), 1988. *Developing world land transport.* Grosvenor Press International, London.

Heraty M.J.(editor-in-chief), 1989. *Developing world transport.* Grosvenor Press International, London.

Institution of Civil Engineers, 1987. *Moving people in tomorrows world; Proceedings of conference organised by ICE, October, 1986.* Thomas Telford, London.

PTRC, 1991. *Urban transport in developing countries.* PTRC, London.

Rogers L.H.(editor), 1986. *International statistical handbook of public transport 1985-86.* UITP, Brussels.

Thomson J.M., 1983. Towards better urban transport planning in developing countries. *World Bank Staff Working Paper No.600.* The World Bank, Washington, D.C.

World Bank, 1986. *Urban Transport: A World Bank policy study.* The World Bank, Washington, D.C.

1. INTRODUCTION

United Nations, 1980. *Patterns of urban and rural population growth.* United Nations, New York.

World Bank,1991. *World Bank Development Report 1991.* The World Bank, Washington, DC.

2. BUS SERVICES

Armstrong-Wright A., and S.Thiriez, 1987. Bus services: reducing costs, raising standards. *World Bank Technical Paper Number 68.* The World Bank, Washington, DC.

Barrett R., 1988. Urban transport in West Africa. *World Bank Technical Paper Number 81.* The World Bank, Washington, DC.

Darbera R., 1991. Les transports collectifs a Casablanca, une privatisation trop regulee. *In: Researche-Transports-Securite No.31. 63-73.* INRETS, Paris.

Dimitriou H.T., 1992. Urban transport planning. A developmental approach. Routledge, London.

Figueroa O., 1991. Organisation et fonctionnement des transports collectifs a Santiago du Chili. Bilan de 10 ans de dereglementation. *Series: Transport, Transfert, Developpement.* CODATU/INRETS, Paris.

Fouracre P.R., D.A.C.Maunder and G.A.Banjo, 1988. Urban public transport as a function of city size: the case of Nigeria. *In: New perceptions and new policies. Urban transport in developing countries.* CODATU, Paris.

Godard X., 1991. Politiques de transport urbain en Afrique sub- Saharienne. Synthese de six etudes de case. *Series: Transport, Transfert, Developpement.* CODATU/INRETS, Paris.

Godard X. and P.Teurnier, 1992. Les transports urbains en Afrique a l'heure de l'ajustement. Redefinir le service public. Karthala, Paris.

Gray P., 1990. Public transport planning for Karachi. *Proceedings of the PTRC Transport and Planning Summer Annual Meeting.* PTRC, London.

Henry E., 1991. L'enterprise bresilienne d'autobus urbains: un modele? *In: Reserche-Transports- Securite No.31. 81-89.* INRETS, Paris.

INRETS/CUIDAD, 1985. Transportes urbains et services en Amerique Latine. *Travail presente a l'atelier de researche INRETS/CUIDAD, Quito, July 1985.*

Lashine A., M. El Hawary and C.R.Eastman, 1987. The development and growth of private sector public transport in Cairo. *Traffic Engineering and Control, 397-401.*

Mandon B., 1991. Bilan d'une decennie de politiques de transports a Dakar. *In: Researche-Transports-Securite No.31. 37-46.* INRETS, Paris.

Menckhoff G., 1985. Technological and ownership options of public transport in India. Paper presented in *'Seminar on metropolitan transport in India'* organised by Times Foundation of India, N.Delhi.

Mitric S., 1991. Crisis and recovery: urban public transport in Morocco. *Transportation Research Record 1297.* Transportation Research Board, Washington, DC.

Won J., 1986. Bus cooperative systems in Korean cities. *Transportation Quarterly, Vol 40(2), 277-287.*

3. ARTICULATED BUSES AND TROLLEYBUSES

Kneebone D., 1987. Transport characteristics of Chinese cities. *Proceedings of the PTRC Transport and Planning Summer Annual Meeting.* PTRC, London.

Shanghai Metro Corporation, 1986. Traffic conditions in Shanghai. *Proceedings of the International Mass Transit Association, Washington, DC, 1986.* IMTA, Washington, DC.

4. PARATRANSIT AND TAXIS

Bourgeois F. and F. Piozin, 1986. The 'redheads' of Niamey: an original way of providing urban transport. *Transport Reviews 6(4), 331-346.*

Clymo J., 1989. Roles of conventional buses and paratransit. *In: Developing world transport, 142-144.* Grosvenor Press International, London.

Crook R.A. and J.R.Jones, 1983. The role of the shared taxi in the urban transport scene: a southern African regional perspective. Institution of Civil Engineers, S.Africa.

Fernandez J.E. and J. De Cea, 1985. An evaluation of the effects of deregulation policies on the Santiago, Chile public transport system. *Proceedings of the PTRC Transport and Planning Summer Annual Meeting.* PTRC, London.

Grava S., 1972. The jeepneys of Manila. *Traffic Quarterly, 465-483.*

Kapila S., M.Manundu and D.Lamba, 1982. The matatu mode of public transport in metropolitan Nairobi. Mazingira Institute, Nairobi.

Oxley P.R.,1988. Dolumus and bus services in Turkey. *In: Developing world land transport, 422-425.* Grosvenor Press International, London.

5. BUSWAY TRANSIT

Fouracre P.R. and G.Gardner, 1992. Mass transit in developing cities: the role of high performance bus systems. *Proceedings of the Institution of Mechanical Engineers Conference: The expanding role of buses towards the 21st century, March, 1992.*

Gardner G., P.R.Cornwell and J.A.Cracknell, 1991. The performance of busway transit in developing countries. *Transport and Road Research Laboratory, Research Report, RR 329.* TRRL, Crowthorne.

Lindau L.A., 1987. Bus priority systems in Brazil: from theory and practice. *Proceedings of the PTRC Transport and Planning Summer Annual Meeting.* PTRC, London.

6. RAIL MASS TRANSIT: METROS

Belda R., 1990. Les raisons du success du Metro de Sao Paulo. *Proceedings of the Institution of Civil Engineers Conference: Rail mass transit for developing countries, October, 1989. 295-306.* Thomas Telford, London.

Benitez B.N. and O.Gonzalez Gomez, 1990. The Mexican Experience. *Proceedings of the Institution of Civil Engineers Conference: Rail mass transit for developing countries, October, 1989. 175-188.* Thomas Telford, London.

Dalvi M.Q., 1990. Calcutta Metro. *Proceedings of the Institution of Civil Engineers Conference: Rail mass transit for developing countries, October, 1989. 255-268.* Thomas Telford, London.

Fouracre P.R., R.J.Allport, and J.M.Thomson, 1990. The performance and impact of rail mass transit in developing countries. *Transport and Road Research Laboratory, Research Report RR278.* TRRL, Crowthorne.

INRETS, 1987. Evaluation des metros dans villes latino-Americaines. *Rapport pour le Ministere de la Researche.* INRETS, Paris.

Marchand L., J.Veinberg and F.Guittonneau, 1983. Rail-based urban transit systems. *In French Railway Review, Vol 1(5), 413-431.*

Sperling D., 1981. Caracas metro- a luxury? *In: Transportation Research Record, 797, 27-31.* Tranportation Research Board, Washington, DC.

7. LIGHT RAIL TRANSIT

Allport R.J., 1986. Appropriate mass transit for developing countries. *Transport Reviews 6(4) 365-384.*

Armstrong-Wright A.T., 1986. Urban transit systems guidelines for examining options. *World Bank Technical Paper Number No. 52*. The World Bank, Washington, DC.

Dans J.P., 1990. The Metro Manila LRT System, its future. *Proceedings of the Institution of Civil Engineers Conference: Rail mass transit for developing countries, October,1989. 159-174.* Thomas Telford, London.

Eastman C., 1987. Improvements to the street tram system in Cairo. *Proceedings of the PTRC Transport and Planning Summer Annual Meeting.* PTRC, London.

8. SUBURBAN RAILWAYS

Barrett R., 1991. Nigeria: urban transport in crisis. The World Bank, Washington, DC.

Indian Railways. Bombay suburban railway system: need for new innovations.

Statement by the Minister of Railways, G.Fernandes, 10.9.90.

Ponnuswary S. and G.N.Phadke, 1987. Development of rail based transit systems in India. *Paper presented at the international seminar on urban transport.* Ministry of Urban Development, N.Delhi.

9. TRAFFIC MANAGEMENT

Armstrong-Wright A.T., 1986. Road pricing and user restraints: opportunitiesand constraints in developing countries. *Transport Research, 20A(2),123-127.*

Cracknell J.A., 1989. Traffic management for urban areas. *In: Developing world transport, 73-75.* Grosvenor Press International, London.

Dawson J.A.L. and I.Catling, 1986. Electronic road pricing in Hong Kong. *Transportation Research 20A(2),129-134.*

Gardner G., G.D.Jacobs and P.R.Fouracre, 1989. Traffic management. *Transport and Road Research Laboratory, Overseas Unit Information Note.* TRRL, Crowthorne.

Jones P.M., 1989. Restraint of road traffic in urban areas. Objectives, options and experiences. *Rees Jeffreys Discussion Paper 3, October, 1989.* Transport Studies Unit, University of Oxford.

JMP Consultants Ltd/ Chulalongkorn University, 1988. Bangkok traffic research project. *Transport and Road Research Laboratory Contractor Report, CR 84.* TRRL, Crowthorne.

Marler N.W., 1982. The performance of high-flow bus lanes in Bangkok. *Transport and Road Research Laboratory Supplementary Report, SR 723.* TRRL, Crowthorne.

10. FARES AND FARE COLLECTION

Armstrong-Wright A. and S.Thiriez, 1987. Bus services: reducing costs, raising standards. *World Bank Technical Paper Number 68*. The World Bank, Washington, DC.

Fouracre P.R., R.J.Allport and J.M.Thomson, 1990. The performance and impact of rail mass transit in developing countries. *Transport and Road Research Laboratory Research Report, RR 278*. TRRL, Crowthorne.

11. FINANCING PUBLIC TRANSPORT

Allport R.J., 1991. Transport concessions study - Thailand, a case study. *OECD Conference, Seville 1991*. OECD, Paris.

Augenblick M. and B.S.Custer, 1990. The Build, Operate and Transfer (BOT) approach to infrastructure projects in developing countries. *World Bank Working Paper*. The World Bank, Washington, DC.

Gutman J.S., 1988. Financing urban transport: constraints and options for developing countries. *Proceedings of the International Union of Public Transport Conference, Singapore 1988*. UITP, Brussels.

Lethbridge N., 1990. Private financing of public transport infrastructure. *Proceedings of the PTRC Transport and Planning Summer Annual Meeting*. PTRC, London.

12. INSTITUTIONAL STRUCTURES

Barrett R., 1991. Nigeria: urban transport in crisis. The World Bank, Washington, DC.

Situma L., 1988. Problems of public transport operations and planning in Zimbabwe. *Developing World Land Transport, 426-430*. Grosvenor Press International, London.

Umrigar F.S., P.K.Sikdar and S.K.Khanna, 1988. Measuring the effectiveness of urban bus services in India. *Proceedings of the PTRC Transport and Planning Summer Annual Meeting*. PTRC, London.

13. ENVIRONMENTAL IMPACT OF URBAN TRANSPORT

Faiz A., K.Sinha, M.Walsh and A.Varma, 1990. Automotive air pollution: issues and options for developing countries. *World Bank Working Paper*. The World Bank, Washington, DC.

Halcrow Fox and Associates, 1991. Environmental action plan for Thailand. *Seventh Plan and Regional Transport, Working Paper NO.16, January 1991*. Office of the National Economic and Social Development Board, Thailand.

Transport and the Environment in Developing Countries. *Proceedings of the PTRC Transport and Planning Summer Annual Meeting 1990.*

The Urban Edge, 1990. Air pollution: a growing legacy. *The Urban Edge, 14(7)*. The World Bank, Washington, DC.

The Urban Edge, 1990. Alcohol fuel from sugar in Brazil. *The Urban Edge, 14(7)*. The World Bank, Washington, DC.

15. URBAN PUBLIC TRANSPORT: THE FUTURE

Fouracre P.R., R.J.Allport and J.M.Thomson, 1990. The performance and impact of rail mass transit in developing countries. *Transport and Road Research Laboratory Research Report, RR 278*. TRRL, Crowthorne.

Fouracre P.R., and J.Turner, 1992. Travel characteristics in developing cities. *Paper presented at The sixth World Conference on Transport Research, Lyon, July 1992.*

United Nations, 1985. *Estimates and projections of urban, rural and city populations, 1950-2025*. United Nations, New York.

World Bank, 1991. *Urban policy and economic development: A World Bank policy study*. The World Bank, Washington, DC.

Printed in the United Kingdom for HMSO
Dd 295719 C8 2/93 36145